As Figure 1 shows, IT and the e-commerce explosion has a direct relevance to the future of your business. It is imperative that you understand the various change̱ ̱ ̱ ̱ ̱ ̱ hought processes based on a renev ̱ ̱ ̱ ̱ ̱ ̱ ̱ ̱ əss into your business.

Your discipline of thought

CW00854689

1 Understanding of your ʊʍʌʊ ʊʊʊʊʊʊʊ ʊʊʊʊʊʊ ʊʊʊ ʊʊʊ ̱d its boundaries.

2 A high degree of understanding of the Internet.

3 Willingness to challenge yourself and the business on a monthly basis.

4 A desire to energize your staff.

5 The discipline to manage and control all of the above.

What is a comfort zone and how do I understand my own?

Put simply, a 'comfort zone' is a set of values based upon your previous experiences, be they childhood or later life, that cause you to have false rules applied to the way you behave. For example if your parents were particularly poor, it is likely you may adopt a frugal approach in your life and feel uncomfortable when money runs low. Or, for example, if your family or your friends do not aspire to better themselves in life, this may cause you to believe that there is a ceiling to the level of success that you can enjoy. Comfort zones are not real, they are simply glass ceilings that prevent you from developing personally and professionally in your business.

To help you to quantify your own comfort zone, ask yourself some simple questions. The answers may give you some direction as to where your boundaries lie in respect to your zone of comfort.

1 How do you feel if you are £1,000 or £10,000 or £20,000 overdrawn?

2 How do you feel making short-term losses to get a medium-term return?

3 How do you feel about detail and planning?

4 How do you feel about wanting to be rich?

5 How good do you feel relative to your competitor/s?

6 Can you decide to dismiss someone easily or promptly?

7 If the business is doing badly, do you
   (a) struggle on
   (b) pretend it is not happening
   (c) take prompt action to cut costs?

8 How do you feel about public speaking?

9 How do you feel about acting alone?

10 Do you mind being disliked for short periods of time?

11 How keen are you to learn on a weekly basis?

12 How do you feel about understanding complex subjects?

These are only some of the questions put to you in order for you to define you own comfort zone. In understanding where you are comfortable or uncomfortable around a subject or situation, you are now able to paint a picture of yourself.

Try to write down as many areas as possible where you feel uncomfortable. From this you will be able to devise a list of areas that may restrict or hold you back in the future.

Comfort zones restrict development and glass ceilings are made to be broken.

MOVING OUT OF YOUR COMFORT ZONE

The next step is up to you. In our entrepreneurial lives we have grown to challenge our comfort zones on a regular basis. Promoting ourselves to accept public speaking events to overcome the fear is the fastest and most effective way of extending our comfort zone. At this point we must refer to the many support and training programmes that are available such as the Small Business Service (formerly Business Link) in your local area, if dropping yourself into the deep end is not your preferred method. "If I can then I will" has become the catchphrase of our own personal development programmes.

The continued training and development of the business leader, is the single and most important differentiator that any small business will have.

It is *this* that will give you the natural extensions to the discipline of thought that is needed to succeed in a small business built to last.

This book will help you, the business leader to train yourself in the necessary tools to develop and modify your existing business, to meet continual change and to cope with the variances and new market conditions.

We have divided the book into three parts so that you can take a slow, methodical look at your current business without missing vital background information and training before you launch into unknown territory.

HOW TO USE THIS BOOK

Building Blocks

Each part has a vital ingredient to make your business develop into a lasting one, so read each section and ensure your business has all the necessary building blocks in place described at the end of each chapter. These building blocks have been summarised to ensure your business at a glance has implemented or thought carefully about each point, before moving onto the next chapter. Use the building blocks as a guideline and work slowly through before moving onto the next part.

The three parts have been divided as follows:

1 A new look at your business

PREPARE

The first part has been written to start you thinking about your business in a completely different way than you may have done so to date. You will be able to look at your business with a fresh pair of eyes and prepare thoughts and ideas in a structured way.

The first four chapters will talk about moving out of your comfort zone and accepting fundamental change as the vehicle to create a long lasting business. You will examine your market place and prepare your own value proposition. Only then will you be able to design a 90-day development plan to shape your business.

Later in this part you will be shown the steps to follow to create a secure environment and how to right-size your business correctly. Discovering your jewels, changing old habits and expanding your business will finalise this part and truly prepare you for the new challenges ahead. By completing this part you will be able to move on and start to plan and accept the necessary changes that will inevitably follow.

2 Gaining a competitive edge

PLAN

This second part is broken down into three chapters, which we feel are the three most important strategies for any small business to understand and adopt to increase their competitive edge.

They are Chapters 5 *E-business explosion*, 6 *Focus on the real customer* and 7 *Picking your partners – cultivating your allies*. On successfully completing Part 1 on preparing your thoughts and ideas on your existing business strategy, you can look forward to developing some new strategies, which may well be out of your comfort zone but the information contained should help to overcome any fears you may have.

These three chapters will provide you with enough ammunition to look around your market place and do business in a more dynamic and cost-efficient way. It will give you a management overview of how to initiate e-business and how to make IT work for your business. By looking at e-business first, you can then consider being part of your customer in a way you never imagined by using automated IT. We will then take a detailed look at your real customers, who they are, and how to create quality repeat earnings and increasing order values.

The next chapter discusses the selection of the right partners to support your customers and increase your market place. It will look at formulating a new market vision with these alliances. Finally we will look at the advantages of acquisitions and how a business leader goes about acquiring another business.

At the end of this second part you will have gained enough information to implement and formulate strategy to take your business forward. All that needs to happen now is to deliver the changes in a controlled fashion.

3 Taking hard and fast action

DELIVER

The third part will show you how to take your current business, modify and adopt new changes identified in the preparation and planning areas of this book and deliver hard and fast action through yourbusiness.

This delivery is controlled by a system we adopted called Rapid Change Management and has been successful in all of our businesses when managing change effectively. You will be shown how to get the best results using this system, how to budget and plan your business development. The system will also refresh your finance and accounting knowledge to ensure you have all the grounding necessary to understand how it affects the bottom line.

The chapter moves on to look at driving sales. It will show you how to forecast and estimate accurately, which is always a major obstacle for any sized company. How to plan your development business over and above your base and then review your sales team and techniques on increasing sales performance. Finally, in the last chapter, we will look at you as the Market Master. How to create energy in the business, your role as a leader and how to recruit and retain good quality people. You will also be given steps to design an organization/team to ensure you have the right people in place so that your small business is built to last.

As we have stated in our opening paragraphs, businesses that last are the ones that have the desire and ability to keep changing. For it is this constant change that will fuel your future success.

We hope that this book will stimulate you as a business leader to build a business fit for the future and one that is indeed built to last.

BUILDING BLOCK 1

- Understand the world is changing at an ever-faster pace over which you have little control.
- Make decisions and develop a willingness to move out of your comfort zone.
- Understand each decision has a consequence and a new direction.
- Your continued development and training is essential for your business success.
- Embrace new technologies and innovate.
- Challenge your thought processes and business rationale regularly.
- Glass ceilings are there to be broken.
- Take all of the above and disseminate it to your staff.

eye of the storm

Understanding your market place

Time and tide wait for no man

UNDERSTANDING YOUR MARKET PLACE

The promised advancements of the combination of low inflation, high growth global economies with the massive potential of dot.com enterprises is now history. The business models of the dot.com companies failed to deliver products to consumers, who in turn did not accept PC technology into their everyday lives at the rate required.

The energy of this storm has given way to the calmness of dot.com failures and economic slow-down, but it is only a matter of time before the storm whips up again. The only difference this time will be that consumer acceptance will have been proven and the dot.com investment will be based on sane business criteria. We are, in effect, sitting in the eye of the storm waiting for technical growth to resume (see Figure 2.1).

We are in the fortunate position of having time to contemplate, learn from recent history and plan for the future, which is becoming more defined as the months pass.

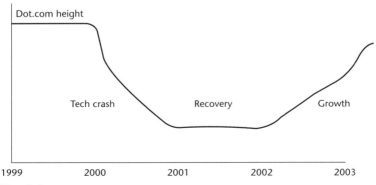

Fig. 2.1

In order to plan effectively, we need to examine some of the impending changes in infrastructure and technology, as they will undoubtedly affect the way we do business in the coming years.

In this chapter, you will learn how to formalize your business planning in all areas to enable you to take decisions from an informed platform. You can never be in the business of 'guessing' the future.

10 steps for stronger business planning

10 steps to strengthen business planning for the future:

1 Understand your market place and ensure your business plan addresses the market issues.

2 Take the opportunity to be innovators as opposed to market followers.

3 Identify partners to create value to your business.

4 Always be customer-led in all of your planning.

5 Be prepared to make radical changes for competitive advantage.

6 Separate your planning into base and development business.

7 Ensure that your plan/model is 'living' ie updated quarterly and rewritten annually.

8 Seek new technologies and apply them.

9 Ensure adequate development and training for all senior staff.

10 Maintain and focus on purchasing within your business.

■ **Step 1. Understand your market place and ensure your business plan addresses the market issues**

Before we look at your business planning, we would first ask you to turn your thoughts to the market place in which you operate. Understanding this market in great detail will provide you with information that will support your growth and continued success.

Before you can gain this understanding it is imperative that you define the market in which you are, or would like to be operating. Be very clear what it is that you sell, and what problems your product or service solves for the customer, as this will direct your market research.

You may think that you are selling a product, whereas the real focus of your attention should be to promote the benefits to the customer as opposed to the product. For example, Amazon having started life as an online bookseller, has identified that its customers, being 'cash-rich, time poor', will also purchase other products such as CD's, DVDs and other easily shippable items. Amazon's market, therefore, is no longer books; it is the provision of leisure media to a defined customer database.

Look long and hard at your market, product and services. Establish what are:

■ the problems you solve for your customers

■ the selling features of your product or service.

Within most markets there exists a trade body, but if not, the local Small Business Service or Chamber of Commerce will assist you in identifying the following. It is strongly recommended that the following list of points are researched on a quarterly basis in order to maintain your company's intelligence as to market shifts and changes.

INCREASING YOUR COMPANY'S INTELLIGENCE

■ The size of the markets in which you operate and the segmentation of sector where appropriate. Each sector has a descriptor code of four digits called an SIC.

■ The major competitors by name, size, time in business, geography, etc. Where these are perceived to be direct competitors, you should also obtain a copy of their financial accounts from Companies house.

■ Website addresses of the known competition, but also perform 'wild card' searches using several different web search engines such as AltaVista and Excite, Lycos, etc.

■ Key factors that prevail in the market place. Understand the shifts and trends of the customer and methods of delivery from other providers. For example, the car insurance market has undergone a paradigm shift in delivery by using the Internet as opposed to high street

---

brokers who often need to cover higher overheads. We have also seen financial services being sold through the major retail outlets such as insurance from Tesco and Marks and Spencer's.

■ The impact of any legislative or technological changes likely in the near future. A large amount of European legislation is expected in the years ahead, which may affect consumer buying patterns or the statutory requirements in the workplace, for example.

■ The customers that are known to buy in this market. By market type, these are often referred to as type A, or AB, or C etc. This classification relates to disposable income and a number of other factors relating to buying habits. Always test your model for the opportunity to amend price or service levels for a different consumer profile.

If this information is not available via the Small Business Service or Chamber of Commerce in your area, then don't forget the trade press periodicals and of course the Internet as valuable sources of research information.

For many small businesses, this vital piece of work is often ignored or neglected, but for the business leader who takes the time to conduct this analysis regularly the benefits can be huge.

From all of the above work, you will have a single theme emerging that describes the market and proposal in one sentence. *This we will term the 'value proposition'.*

Once you are comfortable that you have a value proposition, examine it in detail, and in the context of the above work, find ways to make it as unique as possible. Uniqueness can be found in many forms, from technical advantage, to geographical presence to the methods of delivery. Temporary uniqueness may be found in product features and pricing, but these will be eroded over time.

From this piece of work you will have developed a qualified unique selling proposition that should be short, succinct and communicable.

When you have decided what this proposition is, use it and leverage it in all of your documentation and sales calls. Tell the world, for this is the difference that will convince the customer that you are the supplier for him, and no other.

The point which we have now reached is that we have conducted market analysis and gathered information about the outside world. We have then conducted an exercise to establish our own unique position in the market place: what we now need to do is to establish the link.

We will do this by placing yourself in the context of this market and to try to work out just what are your opportunities and difficulties. The analysis that will now follow is of course the SWOT analysis, which stands for Strengths, Weaknesses, Opportunities and Threats. Take each aspect of your business and perform the SWOT analysis with your team members, and only when you have performed this on every part of your processes from marketing, selling, order handling, delivery process, retention process, planning, management and people (not exhaustive), then you should bring them together and summarise. See Chapter 9 *Driving sales* for a defined process in how to manage change, using teams.

This is a time to be candid and not to fool yourself into thinking that succeeding is a matter of presence. Your competition will not give up the market easily, and for every move that you make, there will be an equal number of people looking at your business to decide how to take you out of the market and the customer base!

*Tip: While conducting the SWOT analysis, ensure that you also decide whether the issues are **present** position or **future** position. This will have a bearing on the weighting that you attach to it later.*

Perform a SWOT analysis to place your company in the context of your market.

From this piece of analysis, you will have reached a detailed understanding of your markets and the ability of your business to compete within it. You may also have researched your known competition to the extent that you understand some of the ways and messages that they use to reach out to the customers.

From the above piece of work, you have conducted a detailed market analysis, and produced a proposition that will prevail throughout your planning process.

■ Step 2. Take the opportunity to be innovators as opposed to market followers

As we are sitting in the eye of the storm, we are able to assess the impact of new technology and how it can be applied to different business situations. It is an opportunity for us to be creative, disregard the rules of yesteryear and to *truly* innovate in our chosen market. When you have done this for the first time, we would recommend that you perform this thought process at least every quarter thereafter.

In order for business to survive, it must be at least as good as most of its competitors. In order for a business to succeed however, it must be better than most of its competitors.

The Small Business Service in the UK promotes benchmarking as a way to achieve best practice. While this has tremendous value in allowing small companies to understand larger businesses, for example, by adopting best practice you can only be as good and not better.

In the 1950s, Boeing innovated with its jet-engined aircraft, while the best practice at the time was propeller-powered aircraft from Douglas. The outcome was of course that Boeing won the day and Douglas remains only as part of Boeing.

In small businesses it can be difficult to truly innovate unless you are in the business of invention or manufacturing. A great majority of small businesses lie in the services or reselling sector. They may find it difficult to envisage a 'jet engine innovation' in their market place. So how do we innovate in small businesses using the eye of the storm as the period in which to implement? The answer of course lies in *convergence*.

Convergence is the bringing together of markets or technologies and the blurring of boundaries between the same. An example is the convergence of commuting and telephony commonly known as CTI. This allows companies to run telephone switchboards and communication routings through computers as opposed to telephone switches. Let us not also forget the WAP Devices (Wireless Application Devices) that are becoming a common theme with the convergence of the mobile telephone and computing based information.

The effect of this is to create more intelligent handling of communications and to reduce costs of transference between these two domains.

The question you must ask is what convergence is or could take place that would apply to my market place?

Answer the following questions to qualify the outcome of your work in this area.

1. Will the changes create competitive advantage?
2. Does this advantage give rise to cost reductions, new technology or technology convergence and market place uniqueness? If not, think again.
3. Do you require partnerships in order to implement? (See Chapter 7 *Picking your partners – cultivating your allies*).
4. Will the changes mean new products or new customers?
5. Is the innovation contained within a 90-day written down development plan which supplements your base business plan? (See 90-day development plan at the end of this chapter.)

■ Step 3. Identify partners to create value to your business

The word 'partnership' conjures up many possibilities depending on the market you are in. Often the concept is already widely accepted, but small companies need partners to survive. What exactly does partnership mean?

We have found it useful to define a partner as follows.

> *Partners are companies or institutions that have ready access to a number of customers who are highly likely to want to buy your product or service. Partners do not usually compete with your offering and, ideally, they see you as complementing or adding value to their own sales proposition.*

While we had a computer hardware reselling business, we established a partnership with a local, similar-sized company that sold commercial telephone installations. The company's installed base showed several thousand customers that could benefit from our product and services. Consequently, we formed a commercial partnership and were able to sell computer networks and services to a new customer base, paying a commission to our partner for each sale made.

So how do we go about finding partners?

Refer to step 2 above and use the market place identifiers to offer clues as to what type of companies would complement your value proposition. Be lateral in your thinking and consider companies or institutions (universities, government bodies, etc) that may initially appear not to have instant synergy with your business.

CHECKLIST: WHAT MAKES A GOOD PARTNERSHIP?

- Most importantly, the culture of the senior management team must be similar to your own.
- The way in which your two organizations treat your customers must be identical.
- The average order of your partner's products must be similar to your own, ie, there is no point in your partner's sales people who are used to selling £500 items recommending your £10,000 service to their client base, as it will simply not be taken seriously.
- Try to concentrate on two or three customers with your partner and prove the selling and delivery processes with hands-on approach with senior management.
- Only when this model is proven, allow your respective teams to take over.
- Senior management must review partners such as these at least quarterly if not monthly, to review the focus and the operations of the partnership.

It is your responsibility as business leader to identify follow-up and secure these partnerships and it should not be left to a less senior manager of your team. We talk about picking your partners and cultivating allies in more detail in Chapter 7 *Picking your partners – cultivating your allies*.

■ **Step 4. Always be customer-led in all of your planning**

It may be obvious but it is as true now as it was 100 years ago—'nothing happens until a sale is made'.

Many small businesses spend a great deal of time trying to work out why a sale was lost. We ask lots of questions of our prospect, which often reveals gaps in our knowledge, which have led to this loss.

How many small businesses actually conduct a win review?

To understand exactly why a customer has purchased from us is to truly understand a formula for future success. We often have little information from our customer base and it is essential that our customers and their needs are accommodated and satisfied in our own planning for the future. Be sure to ask the customer, to share their strategic division of the future with you. You may be surprised to find that your seemingly traditional customer is considering state of the art equipment in their strategic development plan.

If you qualify this point by accepting that your products/services will radically change once every 18 months then you probably will be asking the right questions of your customer.

In the eye of the storm, consulting your customer base and your prospective customers will give an understanding of future spending plans and allow you to plan your business resource levels accordingly. When planning, allow for the fact that the cost and resource associated with selling to an existing customer are a fraction of those required to find a new customer. For a more detailed look at managing the customer relationship to ensure your business is built to last, see Chapter 6 *Focus on the real customer*.

■ **Step 5. Be prepared to make radical changes for competitive advantage**

As the business leader, the hardest decision is to make radical changes to existing business, which often means staff, and resource cuts. We have on many occasions in our business lives, been faced with agonizing decisions to reduce our workforce or cut resource. It is the most natural instinct for many of us to avoid these decisions. However, it is the business survival and the ability for you to live to fight another day are the most important points to consider. See Chapter 4, *Embracing the risks*.

As you move out of the eye of the storm, you may well be faced with the decisions such as these. Your planning process must take a logical approach to the radical changes that may be required for your future success.

■ **Step 6. Separate your planning into base and development business**

If you were to do nothing different in your next fiscal year, and kept the same delivery processes, same overheads, and the same customers (no new ones) then this is described as your *base business*. Base business has a tendency to decline rapidly over time which is why your business constantly searches for new customers to increase or maintain your turnover.

Every activity that you perform over and above this base business, whether that be new customers, new products or services, is called *development business*. It is essential that this development business is measured separately to your base business as a series of projects.

Far greater control, therefore, can be exercised over your development business and the new products and customers than if you simply lump the whole lot together in a single grandiose plan. In a single plan, it will be impossible to understand whether it is your base or development business that is causing sale failure or success.

For more information about implementing base plus development planning, see Chapter 9 *Driving sales*.

■ **Step 7. Ensure that your plan/model is 'living', ie updated quarterly and rewritten annually**

This point is self explanatory as the importance of maintaining current and up-to-date information by which you take decisions cannot be stressed enough. As an aid to this process, see *90-day development plan* at the end of this chapter, which discusses the use of written development plans by you and your team in all aspects of your business.

This process drives both speed and accountability into your company as we pass out of the eye of the storm.

■ Step 8. Seek out new technologies and apply them

New technologies in their various forms, whether IT or market specific, are well documented in such places as national papers, market place periodicals, etc. This information is well worth collecting and considering in your planning processes as discussed above.

Before you rush out and get very excited about the latest 'whiz bang', a word of caution. *Commerce is often very good at over hyping the next two years and underestimating the next ten.* This was evident in the dot.com era in the late 1990s as the two-year horizon failed to deliver to expectations.

Never forget if you are delivering to the consuming public that technology acceptance and its mass take-up often lags behind that of a business. See Chapter 5 *E-business explosion* for detailed analysis of how your business can adopt new technology for commercial gain.

■ Step 9. Ensure adequate development and training for all senior staff

The most important training plan in a small business is the one that many small businesses overlook entirely—the business leader's business plan. If there is no time or resource for the business leader to train, develop and grow then what chance has the business got in the fast changing world that we live. See Chapter 10 *Market Masters*.

A training plan to a business leader needn't necessarily be a formal course, although these have their place. It can also be considered as seminars, networking forums, business clubs and even reading books such as this one, in order to develop the mind and stimulate the grey matter to perform at a higher level. It is also essential for the business leader to have a sound working knowledge of personal computers and such applications as Word, Excel, e-mail and the Internet browser.

Consider joining support organizations, such as the CBI, IOD and your local Chamber of Commerce who are able to provide regular learning material, benchmarking and training opportunities.

Take every opportunity to cross train people in multi-disciplinary, cross-functional and interdepartmental teams. Special effort should be made to eliminate layers of management (not people),

but to speed decision-making and therefore implementation of these changes.

■ Step 10. Maintain a focus on purchasing within your business

> *It is easier to save a pound than to make one.*

It is essential that a small business contain its costs, particularly when it is growing. As we emerge from the eye of the storm, it is those businesses with the lowest cost structures and proportional overheads that will reach their maximum potential. As the business leader you must maintain a watchful eye over your monthly overheads and take a personal interest in constantly seeking to reduce costs. See Chapter 3 *Securing the foundations* and Chapter 8 *Rapid change management*.

We started this chapter by discussing the eye of the storm that gave you the opportunity to plan; we have not so far discussed the form of that plan, which may differ from business to business. Over the years we have produced our planning in many formats from detailed, written-down business plans to simple spreadsheets with a list of assumptions.

Important as business planning is, it cannot be allowed to consume your time to the point that you are less effective as a business leader.

90-day development plan

The concept of the 90-day development plan is vital to the small business leader who aspires to become a market master. Planning is very often put to one side in small businesses, as the daily business consumes the leader's time. By using written-down planning, with a time horizon of only 90 days, then it is possible to focus on the important things only. Ask the question, 'What will I do in the next 90 days to make things better?' Whatever you write down will become the key objectives for the next 90 days. Everything else is subsumed. Try asking your team to do the same thing. Not only will you now have a highly focused team, but you as the business leader will have sight of the planned actions from all of your team, and then you can measure it.

Written-down 90-day planning, adopted by the top team, dramatically increases the chances of success for a business. Use it and encourage its use, as the results are instant, and the effect is polarizing.

BUILDING BLOCK 2

- Understand your market place and ensure that your business planning addresses the market issues.
- Take the opportunity to be innovators as opposed to market followers.
- Identify partners to create value to your business.
- Always be customer-led in all of your planning.
- Be prepared to make radical changes for competitive advantage.
- Separate your planning into base business plus a number of development plans.
- Ensure that this document is 'living', ie updated quarterly and rewritten annually.
- Seek out new technologies and apply them.
- Ensure adequate development and training for all senior staff.
- Maintain a focus on purchasing within your business.

securing the foundations

Shaping the existing business

How to control and deliver

The critical difference between our businesses, is the quality of their leadership. Where the leadership is right, everything else follows. It is the critical differentiator

(Sir M Sorrell)

In a small business that is built to last, we must first recognize that the basics need to be in place before we can start to develop and implement future strategy. In this chapter we will look at how to secure and shape the current business model and build foundations to last.

SHAPING THE EXISTING BUSINESS

This chapter will now cover all aspects of what the business leader needs to focus on in order that the small business is as competitive as possible to accept the challenges ahead.

Create a cash-positive environment

■ Collect your debts

This may sound perfectly obvious, but so many businesses automatically agree to extend payment terms, or simply accept the lame excuse that the cheque run has been missed. The average debtor days should not exceed 48, (assuming your creditors are never paid faster than your debtors), if you want to create a cash-positive environment.

Treat the collection of debts as a serious activity and focus some of your time as the business leader to ensure satisfactory result. In our business, we employed an extremely tenacious, young and enthusiastic individual for this task. Her 'no nonsense, tell it how it is' style made her few friends, but always gained a result when accounting departments tried to delay payment. Our business would never have sustained growth year on year, had this function not been correctly managed.

■ Retention of payments to suppliers – better terms

It's amazing how often you can ask for and get the right payment terms for your business. When your business is new, or recently established, suppliers often ask for cash upfront, or cheque with order. Instead of mumbling a form of agreement with their request, try suggesting that this arrangement is not good for continued business, and that you propose that a 30-day post-dated cheque be used in the first order, and a credit account for net 30 days be established thereafter. (Net 30 days means that you pay for the goods 30 days after the end of the month of delivery. If you take delivery on the 1st of the month, you will pay for it almost 60 days later.)

If you sound bullish enough, the deal is done. As you grow, your new supplier can be told that you simply never pay up-front, and that a net 30-day invoice arrangement is the only way to get your business.

Control of internal and external costs

If you have been in business for a while, and particularly if you employ staff that have authority to spend or commit the company's money, it will be highly likely that your business may have overheads, costs or commitments that you might be well able to do without. To conserve the cash in your business, it is imperative that you control your purchases and points of purchase. Even if you and you alone control the company spend, there will be ways of saving money and therefore maximizing the cash available.

Consider this question: How much is a litre of petrol? It sounds simple, and if you know the answer, then we'll ask you another: How much is the cheapest litre of petrol, and do you buy your fuel at this garage every time you need to fill up? The reason we ask these questions is to illustrate the point that the variance between the cheapest litre and the most expensive litre in the UK is around 15 pence. If your car takes, say, 50 litres in a tank, that difference can be multiplied up to £7.50. If you use one tank per week, this becomes a huge total of £390 in a single year. If you run more than one car, or use more than one tank per week,

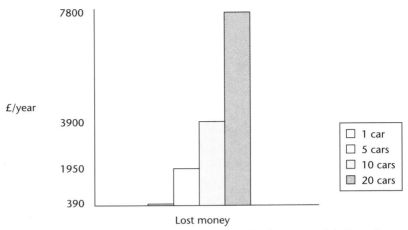

Fig. 3.1 ▪ Effect of using higher priced fuel when a multiplier of many cars is used.

this figure becomes a frightening total representing a significant waste of cash.

Figure 3.1 is a simple illustration to underline the point made above. Every business must reduce and continue to contain overheads to maximise the cash available for working capital.

▪ Have daily cash forecasts in place

By understanding the cash position in written form, and updating this daily, you will have a factual reminder of the available cash to the business. Even when one of our businesses was turning over £6 million, we still required a written cash position on a weekly basis, along with a week-by-week forecast of the bank position over the months to follow. Only by understanding this could we control the stock levels, and the authority to buy for stock. When cash became tight, the authority to buy for stock was removed; when cash was available, we maximized profits by spot purchasing.

▪ Keep the stock to an absolute minimum

The stock in your business may vary from raw materials to general supplies or sub-components of your finished goods. By any other name, your stock is dead cash. View your stock holding at the same moment that you view your bank balance, as the two are very closely linked.

In your business, make sure that your stock turns regularly, and that any slow-moving items are liquidated for breakeven on a periodic basis. Liase with your suppliers, as the reasons for your holding the stock as opposed to your supplier delivering on a just-in-time basis may have been forgotten over time, or simply not explored at all. Incentivize your sales team to clean out the stock items from time to time, and make absolutely sure that your company never buys an item without checking the existing stock levels first.

■ Defer any pay rises

When times are hard in terms of cash flow, and your staff annual pay review looms over the horizon, it is tempting for the sake of retention of staff to simply award the pay rise, as you would like to do. This action will exaggerate the cash shortfall every month and you may wish to consider other means. It is not uncommon to have an open discussion with your team, and perhaps to find a way of deferring the pay rise until some months later. For example, your intended 4 per cent pay increase could be restructured to a 5 per cent rise but effective in 6 months' time. In this way, the award has been made, the employee remains motivated and loyal, and the business has reduced its overall cash outflow for the critical months.

Of course, there are other ways of making package increases. Consider the many elements that go towards making employees satisfied with the company that they work for: such factors as training, pension contributions, health care, parking spaces, and don't forget the employees' personal interests. All of the above may be paid to the employee, although the issue of benefit in kind tax liability may be relevant in some of these cases.

Our advice is to be creative when you are growing a business and are faced with cash-sapping pay reviews. Consider the often forgotten national insurance gain by not awarding the package increase in gross salary, and make sure that your business can afford the pay review in the first place.

The characteristics of an existing business, particularly when you have had a run of success, usually mean that your confidence of further high growth is boosted. You may fail to consider the possibility of a slow-

securing the foundations

down in growth, and as a consequence allow the overheads in terms of salaries to rise beyond a sensible level.

Be careful of using the promotion mechanism in a small business. The title award is a very powerful one, and can often give rise to confusion amongst staff, and loss of focus at a time when it is most needed.

■ Control the telephones and mobile phones

Particularly if you are a service business, it is likely that your telephone costs will represent a significant outlay in percentage terms. In our business, we would reassess the telephone systems and, more importantly, the service provider on an annual basis. As technology improves, the possibility of making large savings by using independent telecom carriers becomes common.

Mobile telephones can be a huge drain on company resources, and are often the emotional issue that no one likes to tackle. In a small business, these loose ends drain cash faster than most, and must be tackled. All mobiles have a printout of the numbers used and the times of the calls, and asking the user to attach this printout with his or her expense claim is a good way of instigating a subtle control without causing a fuss.

Presenting the balance sheet

The presentation of your balance sheet is incredibly important and often overlooked by small business. It is the document by which your financial strength is judged and lending risks are assessed. If you are a business leader who is less then comfortable about financial management then do something about it. *The Small Business Handbook* (Webb and Webb, Prentice Hall 2001) describes financial management in graphical and easily understood terms. Build on this for a more formal understanding as it is a key life skill for the business leader. Contrary to common belief, the balance sheet may be changed and restructured quite legally in order to present the company in the best possible light. In the paragraphs that follow we have suggested some of the obvious ways for you to consider but a competent accountant will offer you such specific advice as your business requires.

The most obvious lender who will assess your balance sheet is your bank manager. It is essential that you shop around and select your bank based on your potential relationship with a flexible and informed bank manager.

Based upon an increasing turnover, you should expect to negotiate an increased facility by the judicious use of cash flow forecasting. This can become the lifeline to your business in times of hardship, and spending time with your bank, enabling them to gain an understanding and trust with you and your business will pay dividends in later times. If your bank fails to share your enthusiasm for your business, then change banks. In a small business you can ill afford the bank relationship to hold you back for no good reason.

This may sound like a glib statement considering the amount of complex debits and standing orders that relate to your account. If you change banking relationships, you will find that all of these details can transfer almost seamlessly. In other words, your new bank should perform all of the set-up instructions on your behalf.

There may be significant pressures from the banking institutions to ask you to consider invoice discounting or factoring as an alternative to the straightforward overdraft or fixed loan arrangements. While these can be of huge benefit to some businesses, it may not be right for yours. Consult your accountant before you make these decisions, and understand the conditions by which you can terminate these arrangements in the future.

■ Using leases to retain cash, as opposed to purchasing assets

From time to time, your business will need to invest in assets such as plant and equipment or motor vehicles. Be aware of the different options available to you financially. Instead of tying up valuable cash which could be used elsewhere, look at the possibility of using a lease arrangement to fund the purchase. This way, you simply lay down a deposit, and commit to a repayment plan over a period of time. In some circumstances—using a rental plan, or an operating lease arrangement—you needn't end up owning the equipment at the end of the period. Again, consult your accountant for the advice relating to the various funding methods open to you, and our advice is to carefully consider any options that will maximize the cash available to the growing business.

■ Sale and leaseback of existing assets

It may well be the case that you have been in business for some time, and that you already own assets for which you have paid cash. In our own business in our fifth year, we had around £30 000 worth of IT equipment, which was bought and paid for in cash. At one time when the cash was tight, we negotiated what is termed a sale and leaseback of this equipment.

This was the sale of the entire IT assets to a leasing company of choice for the same amount as was on the balance sheet. We then signed a lease agreement for the same IT equipment and entered into a structured repayment plan. The equipment did not, in fact, leave our building, and the operations of the business did not change. The net effect was that our business received a cheque for £30 000, and our payments became around £3000 per quarter. The prerequisite is that your balance sheet shows sufficient creditworthiness to sustain this financial transaction, as any leasing company will tell you.

■ Maintain the strongest balance sheet possible

In a small business, you will often be asked for copies of your accounts and balance sheets, to increase supplier credit or to support a large customer deal, which requires you to be vetted financially. This is likely to occur often in a high-growth business, and becomes very common in a small company.

The rules of accounting, although well defined, are in fact open to interpretation with reference to an individual business. We advise you most strongly to understand, by working with your accountants, the various factors that can affect the balance sheet.

The most obvious factor is of course the profit and loss account. The decision of whether to maximize your profits for the business or to minimize them to reduce the taxation burden is a fine balancing act. You must be the judge of the effect on your own business, and the future position once your accounts are filed.

Other factors that can strengthen a balance sheet quite legitimately include the following.

- The policy relating to depreciation of assets. If the depreciation is taken over, say, five years as opposed to, say, three, the write-off to the profit and loss account will be reduced and therefore you will show higher profits.

- The treatment of assets generally if, for example, you group several low value items together and record them as assets rather than writing them off to the profit and loss account.

- The treatment of expenditure that is development work but will be used to make future profits. If you can prove this with a written plan, it is possible on some occasions to capitalize these as intangible assets. This will have the effect of increasing profits, and strengthening total assets on the balance sheet.

- Using rental equipment instead of purchasing or leasing will leave the costs to the monthly profit and loss, and will not show as a liability on your balance sheet.

There are other ways that are more complicated; these we leave for you to explore with your accountant.

Board control

In any small business, the most critical factor that will affect your ability to survive is your management ability. The needs of the business change so fast that you must almost run to keep up.

The strength of the board or senior partners is vital. If the board lacks clarity or doesn't understand finance well enough, your business may well be heading for the rocks.

Examine your board make-up for the following points.

CHECKLIST: BOARD MEETINGS

	Yes	No
Board meetings are held monthly.	☐	☐
All meetings are minuted accurately.	☐	☐
The agenda is issued a week in advance.	☐	☐
The company secretary is well versed in the Companies Act 1985/89.	☐	☐
The directors are all aware of their fiduciary responsibilities in law.	☐	☐
Monthly management accounts are prepared and examined.	☐	☐
All directors understand how to read the profit and loss statement and balance sheet.	☐	☐
Monthly cash-flow model is prepared.	☐	☐
The board receives reports in detail from the following departments: sales and marketing, fulfilment department or manufacturing, accounts department, other vital function departments.	☐	☐
The managing director prepares and submits a report to summarize the month past, and the month in hand.	☐	☐
The use of non-executive directors or board advisors has been considered to add experience to the board from outside the business.	☐	☐
The directors have all attended at least one external training course in the last 12 months.	☐	☐

Key staff retention

Retention of your staff is highly desirable in your small business as they are the key to building a business to last. In our small businesses, it became vital to recruit correctly first time, and so much so, that our management teams were all asked to take formal recruitment training to increase our chances of success.

The structure of your business will become very important on a quarterly basis as opposed to an annual one. In our own businesses today, we frequently reappraise our management lines, teams and focus of our businesses in order to maintain a positive environment for the team to operate in during a sustained period of either growth or consolidation.

When you grow your business, it is critical that you do not succumb to the temptation to promote the longest-serving member in order to 'repay' the loyalty to your business. Too often, we have seen this happen and almost always it ends in tears. See Chapter 10 *Market Masters* regarding the recruitment of people.

There is always, in any business, what we will call the 'core staff'. These are the people who were there at the beginning, or close to the beginning. They are the individuals who will always remember you as one of the team, the person who started out driving the old second-hand car, and who worked the business 24 hours a day.

As your business grows, you will employ more people, who will not become core staff. They will want to work for the company, and not for you. They may well work the numbers of hours for which they are paid, and want to go home at 5.30, for instance! The ability to recognize that this is not their weakness, and is something to be accepted, is often difficult. In a small business, this can often become irksome, and the cause of stress for you. Our advice is that you understand this manifestation, and learn to control it, whilst keeping an eye to the core staff.

Maintaining supplier relationships

Always look to increase working capital by finding new suppliers.

In a small business, the amount of operating cash that is available to the business must become a major preoccupation on a monthly basis. In our business, we regularly recontacted our suppliers and requested higher credit limits, whether or not we needed them at the time. In addition, we always had a practice of increasing the number of suppliers to our business, even if we did not use them often.

What was the point of this? Well, it is quite simple. When the business grows rapidly, there will inevitably be a time when a customer payment fails to arrive on time, or a particularly large deal comes your way. Whether it be the positive or negative factor, the result will be the same.

By increasing the credit limits as above, you will be able to continue to trade and purchase goods to sell while waiting for your debts to be paid.

Ensure customer focus in your business

As we mentioned in Chapter 2 *Eye of the storm*, the difference between you and your competitor is the people you employ. It is important, therefore that all your team, including yourself, have an enthusiasm and alertness when dealing with all customer communications as it could make the final difference between being awarded a contract or not.

Good customer relationships generate repeat business and as we have already stated, it costs far less to retain old customers than to attract new ones.

We have found in all of our business experiences that people buy from people who they like and therefore price is secondary. It is true to say, that we have been in the position with various customers who have asked us to modify our proposal to compete with other offerings in order to justify their decision to place their business with us, as their preferred supplier.

Customer satisfaction is all part of the sales process and the way you interact with your customer has a major influence in the success of your business. Your team has to be totally focused on the customer and their needs.

A disinterested team member will not generate interested customers to your business.

In our computer services company, we operated an excellent customer service programme, which in our industry was second to none. We reaped financial reward in the nineties recession as our company grew threefold while our competitors were pushed to the wall.

Customer satisfaction surveys and customer win/loss reviews identify whether you and your team are successful in giving what the customer really wants. Being close to your customer ensures that you understand their future strategy, which will also aid you in understanding your market place and where to focus your future development of services/products. See Chapter 6 *Focus on the real customer* for more information.

■ **Understand and find your value proposition**

It is essential that you undertake sufficient research to find out what market you are in and what you are actually selling. Please see Chapter 2 *Eye of the storm* to remind you how to conduct this analysis. Once you have qualified your value proposition you can use it to leverage all of your documentation and sales calls.

■ **Ensure the business' IT is sufficient to compete with your major competitors**

Do not be left behind, because your competitors will think nothing of gaining the competitive edge first

Replace computer systems if your business can afford to do so. See Chapter 4, which will offer ideas on how to get the most out of the new technology. Look at implementing the following if you haven't already done so.

■ Link computers and systems to yourself, your suppliers and your customers.

■ Accepting technology will mean accepting changes in the company on a regular basis.

■ Automate processes wherever possible to be cost effective and competitive.

■ Train all staff on software programs, e-mail, Internet, etc.

HOW TO CONTROL AND DELIVER

In small businesses, there are three things that will act as foundations to deliver an impact on how you control your business. These are:

1 *Continued training and development of the people driving the business.* The continued development of the managers of the business (these are the 'top team') is essential if new ideas and greater understanding are to be applied to this rapid change environment. Failure to learn new concepts from any number of sources will rapidly lead to mistakes and lack of opportunities. See Chapter 10 *Market Masters*.

2 *An overt attention to purchasing.* The attention to purchasing is drawn from the fact that it is easier to save a pound than make it, but more than that. The purchasing of materials and assets/consumables of the business is to define the culture of the business. If you are concerned about getting the best deal, this will also reflect in other facets of your business, as well as improve your margins and increase your profits. See Chapter 9 *Driving sales.*

3 *Written-down 90-day development plans.* Written-down 90-day development plans can be extended to all staff within your business. It is simply this: write down a list of things that you yourself will do in the next 90 days in order to make things better. Do this monthly, and gain a rolling set of objectives that recognizes rapid change and drives you to address that change for the better. See Chapter 2 *Eye of the storm.*

These important aspects of control will deliver basic foundations upon which you can now build.

BUILDING BLOCK 3

- Create a cash-positive environment.
- Control of internal and external costs.
- Presenting the balance sheet.
- Board control.
- Retention of key staff.
- Maintaining supplier relationships.
- Ensure customer focus is key to your business.
- Understand and find your value proposition.
- Ensure your IT is sufficient to compete with your major competitors.
- Control the delivery by 90-day development plans.

embracing the risks

Right-sizing the business

The expansion of the business

*Within 5–7 years of its incorporation, a company must create
newness which is greater than what it started with if it is to survive
external conditions*

(A Humphrey)

There are fundamental risks inherent in business whether they be large or small. But due to the volatility of the small business it is particularly relevant that we spend time at looking at two scenarios:

- the right-sizing of the business;
- the expansion of the business.

Both of these situations carry roughly the same amount of risk, which may surprise some of you. The biggest risk however in a small business, is that associated with doing nothing! Doing nothing implies that you are reliant on your base business only and that you have no development business at hand. In Chapter 4 *Embracing the risks* we noted that base business declines rapidly and therefore must be replaced with development business over time.

The mere fact that you have set up a small business means that you are predisposed to accepting an amount of risk. While we are not suggesting you adopt the risks of Boeing when they bet the business in the 1950s by speculatively building the jet-powered aeroplane, we are suggesting that adopting and embracing managed risk is essential to your company's continued development.

The term 'risk management' in commercial terms very often points to people who advise you to reduce your risks and to drive out situations which cause you difficulties within your business. This is of course a path you should follow for unwanted risk or which has little value to your company.

For detailed examination of the management processes, forms and review methods involved in successfully managing risk, see Chapter 8 *Rapid change management*. For direction as to the strategy and options open to you during periods of expansion or contraction then read on.

RIGHT-SIZING THE BUSINESS

How many times do we read in the paper of some big corporation shedding hundreds or even thousands of jobs in the UK? This does not cause us immediately to think that their days are numbered or even that this action is unacceptable. So why is it then, that so many small businesses have an aversion to right-sizing their business to the point where the business leader often risks the entire business in pursuit of other alternatives?

With the acceptance of new technologies and the ability to automate or semi-automate certain tasks, there must be a constant review of any small business of the number of people required to meet the process needs of the company.

For many small businesses, the cost of people can take up as much as 60 per cent of the overheads of the company and maybe even higher in micro businesses. The reduction of this cost therefore, must be highly desirable in order to maximize profits and efficiencies.

Of course, the opportunity to reduce physical costs in the light of technological savings happens rarely in small businesses. It is more common that other factors affect us in business such as a fall in customer orders, cash flow problems or a fundamental market change that impacts the business.

Why consider right-sizing?

Issues that could cause you to question the size of your overheads against the opportunity include:

■ lower than expected sales;

■ degradation of gross margins;

- poorly managed cash flow;
- business making losses;
- fundamental market changes.

Before we discuss these in detail, we would like you to undertake a mind-shift. It is simply this:

Every business in the world, no matter how big or small, complex or simple, partnership or plc, operates on the following terms:
Sales less materials = gross margin
Minus the overheads = resultant profit or loss
The profit or loss is sustained by a cash flow from its previous trading periods or by new money introduced, both of which have a limit.

See also Finance and accounting in Chapter 8 *Rapid change management.*

Separate your business from its products, its services, its commitment and people – what is the primary function of your business now?
The answer of course is to generate cash!

■ Lower than expected sales

- Plot your monthly sales on a line graph to understand if this is a trend or a one-off. Look at ratios such as sales turnover by sales person.

- Review your sales processes against those of your competition, eg level of contact within a customer or use of innovative pricing methods to win business.

- If sales drop against your budget for two consecutive months, this is a trend and requires immediate action.

■ Degradation of gross margins

- This is a measure of gross sales less the cost of the materials which gives rise to the resultant gross margin.

- Higher purchase costs will lead to a lower gross margin.

■ Lower sales costs will lead to a lower gross margin in real terms, ie £100 sale with £30 cost is a 70 per cent margin, £80 sale at £24 costs is also a 70 per cent margin. The difference is that the first generates £70 real margin and the second generates only £56.

■ Poorly managed cash flows

■ The amount of cash in your bank on the last day of each month is a measure of cash flow.

■ Look for reducing or wildly fluctuating balances over a six-month period to indicate ineffective management.

■ Examine debtor make-up for clues to poor payers.

■ Assess your suppliers for opportunities to extend formal payment terms by agreement.

■ Business making losses

■ Monthly management accounts indicating profit or loss are essential.

■ There is never an excuse for a loss, it is simply a loss.

■ Losses in a month result in degradation to cash flow 6–8 weeks later.

■ In the face of losses, an increased overdraft facility is not a welcome solution.

■ Fundamental market changes

■ Unexpected regulation causing market changes eg, health and safety, working time, minimum wage, etc.

■ Massive street level price changes by manufacturers.

■ Sudden product obsolescence.

We have outlined above some of the symptoms which may become apparent to you in your own business. Left unmanaged, these issues will turn into unacceptable risks, which over time will risk the business itself. Every hour of every day in the UK a business somewhere goes into liquidation for the very reasons we mentioned above. To build your small business to last, you must have a constant eye to the clues that tell you that your business is losing shape, focus, or simply losing money.

Your role as the business leader is to constantly measure, review and plan action when such risks are identified. We strongly suggest that you conduct your review by committing to paper your thoughts, measurements and activities.

This will allow you to look at the information dispassionately and also to share this information if you have a trusted friend or colleague who is able to take an external view of your business.

The overwhelming question of course, is when do we take action, how quickly and for how long?

This is largely a matter for you as individuals, knowing how much you have in the bank and the severity of the situation.

Discovering the jewels in your business

The underlying principle to right-sizing your business is to take an unbiased view of your business with a view to identifying the 'jewels'. The jewels are a euphemism for those aspects, ie processes or people that add the most significant value to your paying customers. Try scoring these on a 1, 2, 3 basis where 1 is the person or process which adds the most value and 3 is something you could do without.

This may be best achieved by involving a third party such as your accountant or a Small Business Service adviser. Try to be objective in your approach, especially where people are concerned, ensuring that friendships, good relations or past performance do not cloud the issue.

If, as in Chapter 3 *Securing the foundations*, you have decided to develop a new strategy for your business, then ensure the values required by these strategies are reflected in your choice of jewels.

As with any set of jewels, this selection will give you the most sparkling chance of success in your future business.

The next step is to test the relationship between the people and the processes to ensure the strategy and direction of your business can be achieved. This is initially best achieved by flow-charting the approach to the customer, order receipt, delivery and support processes. This will identify any gaps.

Having identified gaps, please do not instantly fill it by recruiting another person before you have asked whether this can be done by cross training from within. In small business we all wear many hats and simply because you may have not done something recently, certainly doesn't mean that you won't have to do it in the future.

An example of a business process flowchart is shown in Figure 4.1.

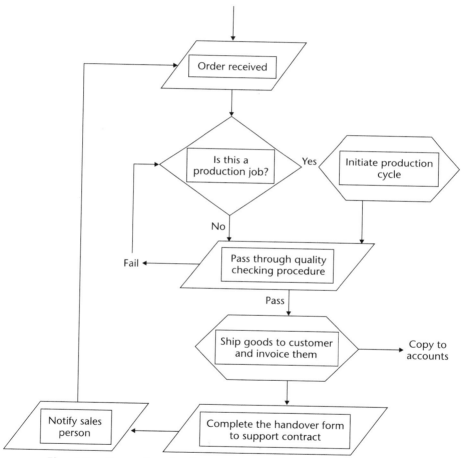

Fig. 4.1 ▪ Example of a flow chart

How far do we go in right sizing?

The answer to this question lies within each individual business, the principle is to build a business to last. We do this by generating sales, delivering orders, collecting cash and cycling. The element here is the cash, in order to ensure your continued survival and that you are able to live to fight another day.

Treat any right-sizing action as a project—this will help you to identify its boundaries, its duration, its desired outcome. It may also assist you in separating the emotion of people right-sizing from the declared needs of the business.

In defining right-sizing as a project, you need to focus on the following areas:

- marketing expenditure;
- optional expenditure;
- building expenditure;
- financials;
- use of IT;
- process re-engineering;
- people.

■ Marketing expediture

This is the area that most small businesses right-size first. For most business leaders it is top of the list when it comes to cutting costs. However, when performed properly, marketing is the art of attracting the attention of new customers and reaffirming the purchasing decision of existing customers.

Marketing drives perception of your company and its market and your presence, whether it is in public relations, editorials, well-presented brochures, or well placed advertisements, will be known in the market place.

Analyze the source of the initial contact with your last 30 orders, as this will tell you how big a role your market function has taken in generating these customers.

For some small businesses the marketing activity in advertising and PR generates the majority of their enquiries and to cancel this expenditure without thought is to compound your problems in the short to medium term.

However, if the marketing spends cannot justify in terms of selling results, then by all means, look at limiting the cost. If you do this we would urge you not to simply forget about it, but to review its impact in future months.

For many of you undertaking this exercise, you might think that your website and continued maintenance and updating may fall in the cost elimination category—we would urge caution here. In the Introduction, we discussed the fact that where the Internet is concerned we have consistently overestimated its progress for the next two years and underestimated over a ten-year period. A well-developed website will act as a high-quality message to existing and new clients 24 hours a day, 7 days per week. A website can also be used to solicit feedback, announce new products and services, act as an information portal and as a statement of presence in the market.

Consider this against a high-quality brochure print with its associated mailing costs and feedback telephone calls and the resultant handling. The website can be a very effective way of enhancing your business in your chosen market and can significantly reduce internal costs along the way. See Chapter 5 *The E-business Explosion.*

■ Optional expenditure

Optional expenditure exists in every business. As the term suggests, these are the items of spend that you can run your business without. To give you some examples, in our own businesses, magazines and periodicals, convenience stationery, office decoration, gifts, entertainment, unnecessary capital equipment, all fall into this category.

Does your business enhance its sales or profitability with a direct link to one of the above? If the answer is no, then try eliminating these costs.

This is not a one-off exercise, as during any period of success, optional purchase requests will be made, which means that you have to constantly review optional purchases on a quarterly basis.

■ Building expenditure

'Building expediture' refers to the actual costs relating to your business premises, such as rent, or mortgage plus business rates and of course the associated utility running costs. In a right-sizing business, it is important that you do not go on running large premises needlessly. If you operate a multi-level building, ie you occupy more than one floor, by consolidating to a single floor you may achieve local business tax relief for the unoccupied space.

Additionally, you may be able to sublet any surplus space to another small business. It is important to involve a solicitor in formalizing any arrangements as you do not wish to compromize your existing lease or mortgage contracts and you need to retain the power of eviction if you so wish.

When you right-size a business, it can be an emotionally stressful time for all of your team, and rearranging the format of your office may be advantageous to instil comradeship among your team.

If you are looking to relocate to smaller premises, examine your break clauses in your lease and make yourself aware of your legal obligations. Don't simply accept the terms of the lease without question, but rather, take a meeting with your landlords, explain your position and ask for their assistance to achieve your needs.

There are many reasons why your landlord may wish to accommodate you, not least because a higher market rent may be available to them with new tenants.

With regard to utility running costs, this section will even apply to those who run businesses from personal premises. It is a common belief that utility charges associated with electricity, gas, water and telephone are pretty much fixed. This is simply not the case. There are very many deals available to small business since the deregulation of the utility markets which allow significant savings to be achieved using a single carrier.

The telecommunications market is even more open with respect to your choice of carriers, along with things like 'least cost routing'. This is an arrangement whereby a combination of hardware and software automatically routes your call around global networks, resulting in the cheapest unit per minute price to your business.

In addition, remember that your method of payment can affect your costs in these areas, and whether you choose monthly direct debit, quarterly invoice, or monthly in advance will affect the price you pay. Make sure you consult with your local chamber of commerce in the matter of utilities as they very often use the bulk purchasing power of their extensive small business membership to negotiate corporate-style deals for your benefit.

■ Financials

There is a cost to maintain the financial information in any small business, which is determined by your turnover. In the UK, for example, there is an audit exemption level under which small businesses are not required to pay for an audit, but simply to file accounts to Companies House. Contact an accountant for further advice.

Additional financial costs relate to debtor management, ie the collection of debts from your customers. If you find this difficult, consider outsourcing it to firms that specialize in the recovery of outstanding invoices. Outsourcing can remove the overhead, telephone calls and frustration, trying to recover money and free you to get on with core business.

You might also consider, in consultation with your accountant, the opportunity to use factoring or invoice discounting companies that will advance up to 80 per cent of the invoice value within, say, 10 days of you issuing your invoice. The result of this will be the availability of cash within your business, particularly in the first month of its operation when the factoring or invoice discounting company buys your debtor base and immediately releases up to 80 per cent of its value in cash.

Preparing monthly accounts, including VAT, reconciliation, tax calculations, payroll and generating relevant reports is a service that you may consider outsourcing to an accountant. Consider the costs of this against the cost of employing a qualified financial person and the possible benefit of regular and accurate accounting information to run your business.

■ Use of IT

Efficient communications are essential for small businesses and the use of web-based mail, and web-based faxes will produce flexibility in your new operation.

You should also consider the access you have to important information such as customer data bases or technical information, and look hard for, those manual processes that compensate for inefficient or disconnected IT functions.

Analyze your methods of telecommunications and seek out a supplier or carrier who allows you to bring together land-based telephony, mobile-based telephony, e-mail and fax into a single domain.

Creating the IT and communications environment that is joined up, fit for purpose, frees people to interact with other people and provides a platform for success.

Covered in detail in Chapter 5 *E-business explosion* are the opportunities to link your IT systems to those of your customers and suppliers. This will have enormous benefits to your business in so far as it allows more corroborative business to take place, while at the same time stripping out costs usually of manual processes which normally interface with your customers and suppliers.

■ Process re-engineering

In the sections above, we have referred many times to process changes that can remove costs within your business. The most common types of process are customer communication, order receipt, organizing the order and delivering an invoice. If you have been in business for some time, it is highly likely that your business does not adopt the most efficient system for handling these.

When right-sizing your business, consider how your suppliers can assist you to increase the efficiency of your preparation for delivery process.

There are also potential savings to be made by using a call centre to accept your incoming calls and then transferring either the call or the message to the person who is best able to handle the information. Call centres answer calls professionally and consistently, do not go sick, do not have absences or holidays and provide a standard interface for your customers and suppliers alike.

If you choose to investigate this route, make sure you visit the call centre and speak to a number of their reference sites and ensure that the call centre can interface with your telephony system, your mobile telephones, your e-mail systems and your website (whether this is relevant to you or not).

The use of a call centre can also allow you to extend your company's perceived working day from 9am – 5pm to 7am – 7pm or even to 24-hour call receipt, for a relatively low cost. This may have a bearing on your value proposition in Chapter 2 *Eye of the storm.*

In your business you may find certain services or equipment is finan-cially contracted over a number of months or years; when assessing your business processes do not be constrained by the contracts that relate to the above items. Always try to negotiate with the contract holder for the outcome you desire. In our own businesses we negotiated the return of a surplus to requirements photocopier with only a small, agreed severance payment, which was outside the original contract terms.

Similarly we negotiated for the return of two one-year old, three-year-contract cars, in return for accepting a single new car in their place, again, outside the original contract terms.

People

We have left the most difficult part of right-sizing your business to the end of this section. As we stated in the opening paragraphs of this chap-ter, small businesses—through their reliance on relatively few individ-uals—find it much harder to downsize their teams than larger businesses.

Some of the reasons for this might include the following.

- Because the business is small, closer relationships are formed between the business leader, team members and sometimes their families.

- Business leader generates a dependency upon the individual (which is emotive rather than logical).

- Business leader, having worked hard putting a team in place, does not look forward to being perceived as going backwards in his or her decision making.

It is essential that you approach this from a logical and not an emotional direction. Separate yourself from the business and instruct yourself to be objective with your decision making. It is recommended you have a third party such as a business adviser or consultant to advise for the best outcome.

Where do you start?

From the work you have done in the sections above, you will have already discovered by analyzing process and spend, that there may be a small number of team members who are not required for the new business model.

The term we use for terminating an individual's contract in this situation is 'redundancy'. The structure of this in the UK is to pay the employee the notice period, which you are entitled to ask them to work, plus a statutory amount of redundancy pay. The amount of redundancy pay is directly proportional to the employee's length of service and the business leader should consult a solicitor or accountant to quantify this.

For most companies, the employer can improve the redundancy package for the employee by not requiring the notice period to be worked. This is entirely optional.

The process of redundancy must be seen to be considered and fair. In this time of significant social legislation, we would strongly recommend seeking advice from a solicitor to ensure your business acts appropriately—mistakes in this area can be very costly. For example, if you make an individual redundant then fill that position with a new hire soon after, this is seen as running contrary to employment protection legislation.

Obviously every small business is different and whatever we suggest cannot be a panacea for all companies, but to help you focus your mind on what is good for the business. Figure 4.2 shows a common denominator for all small businesses.

Into this diagram, you can now insert the revised strategies from Chapter 2 *Eye of the storm* and the changes you made in Chapter 3 *Securing the foundations* along with the re-engineering and differing approaches you have established in this chapter.

You should find that the outcome is the semi-automation or, where you have outsourced the processes, full automation of parts of your business.

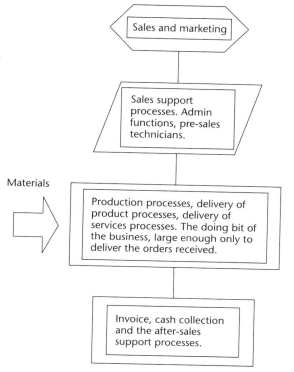

Fig. 4.2 ▓ **A common denominator**

What you now need to do is take all of your people and take them out of your business. By doing this you are simply left with the business requirements and not a decision about individuals. You can now select people from the resource pool in order to meet the needs of the business in its diagrammatic form. Do not compromise the skills set required against the skills set available.

A square peg will fit into a round hole but there will be gaps in all four sides.

At this stage, do not be swayed by length of time in service, personal circumstances or salary packages, this analysis will come later. You may find there are defined roles within your new operation that have no skills match from your present team. This must be clearly identified and a recruitment process started to fill the role.

Who should be retained?

Key attributes to look for when selecting from the resource pool may be summarized as follows:

- enthusiasm;
- commitment;
- intellect;
- ability to accept continuous change;
- skills relevant to your business;
- ability to cross-train in various business functions;
- excellent IT skills.

Remember one thing, a positive attitude is not trainable.

Once you have established the extent to which the resource pool can satisfy the diagrammatic new business, then you must test the team attributes to ensure that the business is able to function correctly. Remember, as we stated earlier, when right-sizing a business we are establishing or accepting a lower turnover changed business model, and the wearing of many hats once again.

As a philosophical point, when right-sizing a business, consider the old company to be closing down and the new company starting up the very next day. It is important to break from the past and understand that your business is built to last, must transform itself and start again.

With this break from the past comes the opportunity to reorganize management structures making them flatter or indeed eliminating them in favour for a direct report. It also allows you to change the rules and to change old habits. See Chapter 8 *Rapid change management.*

THE EXPANSION OF THE BUSINESS

Focus on the strategy

The small business is like driving a racing car. The bends arrive so much quicker than normal, the engine revs faster, and the alertness of the driver is the key to potential success. When your business becomes fast-moving in this way, it is vital that you have a view of what is in front of you.

The strategy of your business and the vision that you articulated in the opening chapters of this book will need to be reviewed regularly. A good perception of the market place and economic factors is needed as well as an 'ear to the ground' with respect to your suppliers and customers.

Factors leading to expansion

In the opening paragraphs to this chapter, we discussed the inherent risks involved in right-sizing and expansion. For many business leaders, the word 'expansion' conjures up thoughts of easier times, manageable cash flows and profits.

There is, in fact, just as much risk in expansion as there is to right-sizing. Before we go on to examine the risks in detail, we will select a number of indicators that describe a business in expansion.

- The business has won a large order.
- There appears to be a trend of increasing sales.
- Existing business processes appear to be unable to cope.
- More people are required within the business.
- The use of effective IT in the business is low.
- Cash appears short despite profitable sales.

There are other indicators, of course, and the list is not exhaustive, but represents some of the common factors that prevent a business from expanding without incurring unacceptably high risks.

Slimming down before building up

Having read the section on right-sizing your business, you will already have noticed that some of these indicators need not be there. The risks, therefore, will be higher for the business that grows with no regard to its present position and thus its future potential.

For example, if you were planning to run in a 26-mile marathon, would you simply get up one day and start the race or would you have spent some time in the weeks and months beforehand, in training, building up your muscles, stamina and race plan? A business in expansion mode usually starts with a symptom like rising sales, it is imperative that it slims down before it builds up. Just like the marathon runner.

By referring to the section above we suggest you conduct the same exercises of cost containment, process re-engineering, outsourcing assessments and personnel skills analysis that you have just completed in right-sizing your business. A business needs to be built on solid foundations and the less than effective processes and approaches in your business must be driven out. A house without a foundation will look pretty for a while until the ground starts to sag beneath the weight of the building upon it.

Funding

During periods of expansion, due to less than perfect debtor collection, or the cash required to fund work in progress, the working capital of your business will come under severe pressure. It is important therefore to forward plan your levels of sales and the amount of resource required to deliver within an accounts-based spreadsheet.

This will inform you of the amount of working capital required and the effect upon your cash flow during this time of expansion. The result may just surprise you and indicate to you that in order to fund the sales your business may require additional cash to sustain its overhead. This situation is compounded when you start to expand your facilities or hire new team members.

Typical sources of funding include the following.

- Extension of your suppliers' credit terms—the cheapest form of working capital available.
- Focus on customer debt collection.
- Small Business Service may offer grants, please contact your local division for further details.
- Factoring or invoice discounting releasing up to 80 per cent of the invoice value within 7–10 days of the invoice being presented.
- Additional funds from the business leader from personal assets.

- Sale of some shares of your company to family members or employees.

- Venture capitalist who may extend larger sums of money but will demand a place in your board structure.

- Private placing—an official way to sell shares to known private investors (plural).

- Public offering of your shares by way of a stock exchange listing.

This list is not exhaustive, but is a comprehensive guide to some of the options available. It is essential that you involve your accountant in this decision and that you interview at least three corporate financial advisers before appointing them. Be sure to speak to Managing Directors of at least three companies of similar size to your own if possible in a similar sector before making this important appointment.

Attention to the customer

It is very common in periods of expansion that the business leader becomes busy doing lots of different things. It is likely you have held close personal relationships with your customers prior to this time. See Chapter 3 *Securing the foundations* for advice about retaining customer focus and Chapter 6 *Focus on the real customer*.

To simply pass this dialogue to the sales department would be to risk the relationship with the customer. It is incredibly important to put yourself in the customer's shoes and either to maintain contact at all costs or to discuss sensitively with your customer the possibility of introducing a trusted person in your company to deal with them.

We speak from bitter experience having lost a highly valued customer as we failed to move the relationship to our sales team with sensitivity. Our customer felt neglected and even snubbed—his perception was that the Director had lost interest and handed his contact to a mere salesperson.

Don't learn this from your own loss—learn it now!

Integrating new people

When your business was first established, it is likely that just a handful of people were working in the company. The team spirit was extremely high and everything possible was done in pursuit of sales success or satisfying a customer need regardless of the day or the time.

As any business grows and becomes more professional, people who do not perhaps share the same core values or beliefs as the founding team add to the core team. It is very important for the business leader to recognize this and make every attempt to break down the barriers and integrate additional team members into the core. This will assist the business greatly as it grows and will lead to a reduction in disputes with individuals in the months and years to come.

Importance of planning

As stated in previous chapters, the control of the business at a time of expansion becomes more difficult. A larger range of variables such as sales, cash, people, processes and maybe funding all add to the complications.

During this period of intensive change you may wish to adopt formal systems which turns the guesswork into a team led process. See Chapter 8 *Rapid change management* for an explanation of how this can work in your business.

BUILDING BLOCK 4

- The biggest risk in a small business is the risk of doing nothing, because you are reliant on your base business.

- Right-size your business immediately if you see a reduction in sales, gross margins, cash flow, or fundamental market shifts.

- Plot your monthly sales to understand trends.

- Review your sales processes.

- Look for ineffective management by looking closely at cash flows.

- Examine debtor make-up for poor payers analysis.

- Assess whether suppliers can extend payment terms.

- Measure, review and plan action when such risks are identified.

- Discover the jewels in your business.

- When right-sizing, look at all expenditure, use of IT, process re-engineering and the people in your business.

- During expansion, understand all the funding opportunities and development plans available to you.

- The rapid change management process can help in right-sizing and expansion of your business.

embracing the risks

gaining a competitive edge

5

E-business explosion

Definitions

The automated workplace

Putting it all together

Technical innovations in the
not-so-distant future

Making it work for your business

"JUST BECAUSE I WANT TO DISCUSS E-BUSINESS"

Most e-business-related books appear to concentrate on very large businesses making very large changes for very large gains. While this stands to illustrate the e-business revolution and what it can achieve from corporations of this size, small businesses are forced to sit back in awe and wonder how they can benefit from the e-business explosion.

This chapter is for the small business only.

The first important thing to understand is that e-business is currently being measured in two forms:

- business to business (B2B);
- business to consumer (B2C).

The statistics for the size of the growth of e-business nearly always enjoy a hockey stick growth profile. But there is a marked difference between B2B and B2C in the coming years, as illustrated in Figure 5.1.

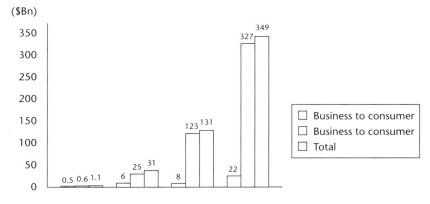

Fig. 5.1 ▦ Internet commerce is growing rapidly

The chart shows the widely different expectations of the growth in business to business services and the business to consumer services. The reason is quite simple. Business to business is quickly able to justify its investment by a reduction in costs, enhancement of speed or improvement to its route to market; in other words, it is great for business.

Business to consumer, however, relies upon you and I and people like us using the Internet at home to buy goods and services. As you can see from the chart the consumer market is a tiny fraction of the business market in the coming year.

Each year the markets try to talk up the acceptance of the Internet in our home and try to push business to consumer services at us. It may surprise you to know, that despite our impression of the global village, 80 per cent of the world population has never even made a telephone call. No small wonder then that business to consumer services will lag behind business to business services for some time to come.

So what does a small business need to understand in order to embrace e-business in a practical and easy way?

The key word for us in small business is 'automation'. See Figure 5.2.

With the advent of Microsoft's range of small business software in recent years, it is possible for very small cost to set up a network to link all of your PCs with a common application suite, common data repository and a gateway to the Internet with an e-mail address.

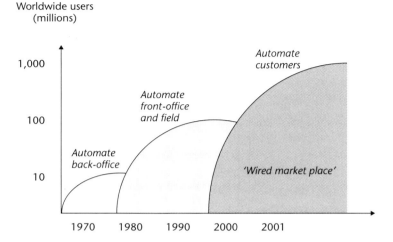

Worldwide users (millions)

1,000 — Automate customers

100 — Automate front-office and field

10 — Automate back-office — 'Wired market place'

1970   1980   1990   2000   2001

Fig. 5.2 ■ The e-commerce revolution

Although these are extremely common terms, for many small businesses nobody has taken the time to explain it properly. The net effect is that we are afraid to ask! The consequence is that we lose competitiveness and opportunities.

It is vital that we as business leaders are able to understand enough of the technologies that will lead to our business automation. It is not essential that you understand how systems work, but merely the questions to ask and the direction to move in. Specialists will supply systems to a business specification set by you the business leader. But unless the business specification is generated by the business leader it can only ever be a long list of technical features.

This chapter will provide you with:

■ a management overview of the tools to initiate e-business;

■ a description of some strategies that you may wish to consider for implementation by your own business;

■ the latest technical innovations about to be launched and the likely impact that this will have upon certain markets.

DEFINITIONS

Below—in no particular order—we will define the various buzzwords that describe how e-business can work in your business. This section is not optional as in the future all businesses will need to embrace, accept and implement aspects of the electronic world in order to remain competitive and build a business to last.

Glossary of terms

To help you in your understanding of the technologies, Figure 5.3 is intended to put into context some of the terms. Please refer to this diagram while reading the glossary.

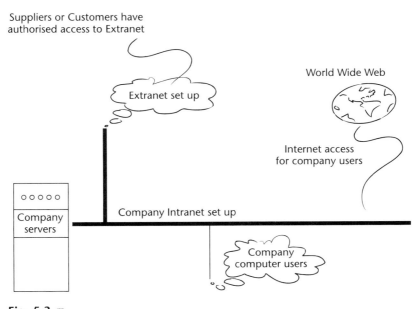

Fig. 5.3 ▦

■ Internet

The word Internet simply describes a global network of telephone lines and satellite communications that are able to link to most points on the globe. Instead of making a telephone call however, the Internet allows any computer, however big or small, to send data or information, pictures sound text and video down the telephone line.

The World Wide Web refers to the hundreds of thousands of computers that form part of today's set-up. As the Internet is simply a huge conglomerate of telephone connections, there is no law regarding the type of information that can be connected to the Internet, so the answer to the question of who owns the Internet is of course, nobody and everybody!

It is this huge richness of different data, information and content, however informative or illegal, connected via computers to the Internet that makes the Internet the highlight of human achievement, and simultaneously the depths of human despair.

Most information is found by associating it with a domain name, which is found to start with www.[name].xxx. This domain name acts as a librarian filing your information where you and others are able to find it. The librarian on the World Wide Web is called a search engine.

It is because the Internet can transfer tremendous amounts of complex and valuable data for the price of a local telephone call that makes it such a revolution and will change the way we communicate on a global basis.

The language of the Internet is known as *html* or *xml*, which is the code that is used to present information on a screen in a pretty and readable format.

Your business can design a website and publish it on the World Wide Web for the world to see. *It is this possibility of 24-hour a day presence that turns the planet into a global village.*

How the Internet affects the way we do business

It is well documented that more business than we can ever comprehend will continue to operate across the Internet, meaning that time and distance will now not affect commerce. As we hear about new net businesses starting up every hour, no small business can afford to neglect the potential.

By opening a site on the World Wide Web, your business becomes automatically international. Through the site your business can:

- inform customers about your products;
- direct sell across the net;
- link up with suppliers;
- sell to a world-wide audience;
- sell via partners;
- link information to your distributors;
- your business' central pricing list/selling documents can be accessed via the net remotely and can be used by your salesperson face to face with your customer.

Some points to adhere to when implementing your IT strategy include the following.

- Excessive internal focus can create more processes and paperwork.
- Limited sharing of information and resources can cause the strategy to fail and not achieve savings to the bottom line.
- The electronic layer to the business could cause additional pressures on your team. If yours is disinterested, it could cause impaired performance.
- This new revolution has reshaped companies in the way they purchase through their business. There is no longer the need for individual purchasers with deep knowledge of markets to be employed. Instead, a few clicks on the mouse will establish best sources of supply and availability.
- Adopting changes mean a new way of doing things—led by IT. It demands a change of attitude from the business leader.

The main difference between business leaders who make the Internet work for them and those who don't is their attitude to its implementation. Until the business leader shows willingness to be open to the sharing of information with all of his or her team, customers and suppliers alike, then the new technology will never truly affect the profitability of the business.

E-business explosion

■ E-mail

'E-mail' is one of the most common terms in business today. Short for electronic mail, this concept uses the Internet to move electronic mail around the world for the cost of a local telephone call . If the World Wide Web content can be indexed via the *www.name.xxx* protocol, then it stands to reason that each person can have an independent address on the Internet as well. If you have a computer then you can apply for an address for yourself usually for free. If you have an address, then you can send private information from you to another individual, just so long as you have their address as well.

Benefits to small business

E-mail as a culture has become commonplace since 1995, with most business people in larger companies having an e-mail address by which they can receive and send electronic information such as documents, spreadsheets, pictures, etc. For it is this aspect of e-mail that makes it a most powerful ally to the small business. The ability to move complicated information by using the e-mail as the train, and the files attached as the carriages, puts you in the same efficiency category as a large corporation.

As a supplier or a customer to you, the ability to quickly send electronic notes or attach pictures or complex files for your easy reading within minutes of sending it, is becoming a necessity and not a luxury.

E-mail will reduce costs and allow your business to adopt a speed that you would never achieve without it. If you don't have an e-mail address today, then go and get one. If you haven't connected to the Internet, then make an appointment with the Small Business Service who will take time out for you to try it for free.

Where e-mail is available to all employees (as it should be in any wired organization), the average person will send between 4–12 e-mails a day and receive perhaps 10–15. A knowledge worker or key executive can expect to receive 100 messages per day and to send around 30.

E-mail is also a catalyst to flattening organizational structures. The less formal tones used when writing an e-mail as opposed to a formal memo, and the ease in which groups of people including senior executives can be automatically copied, promotes open and frequent communications.

E-mail should never be used to send bad news or to make contact with a new client.

As you implement e-mail within your business, ensure that your employees are officially notified of the expected proper use of these systems and consult a solicitor to establish the company's rights in law to randomly check employees' e-mails.

Employment legislation in this area is changing and the company needs to establish the rules from the outset, with a carefully thought-out e-mail/Internet policy.

■ Website

This is the location of content or information that you have published to describe your business, service or other information. The website is written using the html code or xml code that we described above. It should look attractive, engage the reader and not simply replicate your printed brochure.

Website design has become a lot more sophisticated in recent years and the adage that 'what you pay is what you get' certainly applies. The website is not about a youngster putting code together; it is your 24-hour a day advertisement for your business. This is the location to which your largest prospect will visit before they make that vital decision to place an order with you.

Will it be cobbled together by a cut-price offer, or will you put resource and effort into finding a proven website design company which can show you many sites with interesting designs and happy customers? Always obtain references and ensure that you are one of the smaller clients and not one of their biggest.

Before you select your website design, ensure that you spend at least five hours yourself as the business leader, just looking at the Internet. If you don't have your own connection, then your Small Business Service is the next stop for you.

Look at your competitor's websites, examine comparative industries and perform searches using the search engines. Understand just how unstructured the World Wide Web is, and how easy or not it is to find specific information that you require. Challenge the Internet and reach out for the experience; don't be afraid of it, it is only a machine connected to a telephone line, and you certainly cannot break it!

As with e-mail, the use of an Internet connection by employees can invite difficulties. From the outset the company needs to establish its legal framework, which allows employees access to this unregulated medium. Transmission or receipt of pornographic material is illegal in some countries and employees accessing this and other non-work related websites can be detrimental to the business.

Internet security

No section on the Internet would be complete without the stern warning to all users to ensure that adequate security measures are taken. What you pay is what you get here, so don't look for a cheap tick in the box. Each and every user must have virus protection software installed on their machines. We suggest that this is not a one-off exercise, and that a formal responsibility is placed upon all users to ensure the utility is run daily and updated weekly. New viruses appear each day, and so it is worth a little time and effort in this area. When publishing information via a website, ensure that a firewall protects your information. Sites are constantly being hacked and graffiti placed over the front pages. If in doubt, or this is not your strong area, then seek professional help, and remember, this is the lock on your front door; leave gaps at your peril, and don't leave the key in the door!

■ Intranet

This is not the word Internet spelled wrongly! It is a variation of the set-up that allows you to publish information on a server in the same way as the Internet. The difference is that the access to the information and sites is restricted to those in your own company. Why would you do this?

The ability to publish information in the format of a website makes information far more interactive and powerful. You can make text and pictures come to life by making them index links to other information, and all presented over the browser in a rich format. Using special security, it is also possible to allow other sites like your own home or other offices to link up to bring information together in a collaborative and sharing form. It is this aspect that will deliver further savings and efficiencies in the future.

■ Extranet

This is a secure method of access, which allows customers and suppliers of the company to interact with your company's intranet. This cuts out manual processes and makes ordering and enquiries far more efficient in the supply chain. A typical example of this is Federal Express, which allows its customers to order and track a consignment using the Internet.

Your business is able to have multiple extranet arrangements, which can effectively link your suppliers to your customers and automate the communications for order delivery and specification enquiries, for instance.

THE AUTOMATED WORKPLACE

Imagine a world where your business is fully automated. Using technology you are able to link every aspect of the information contained in your business to the people in your business.

Gone are the manual processes of constructing databases, writing proposals, investigating new products. Instead, technology delivers this information in a form that you can easily read, change, drop into templates and deliver to your customer. Customers can obtain quotes, place orders and progress deliveries by connecting directly to your computer systems. Inefficient, time-consuming verbal enquiries will become part of a bygone era as automation provides timely and accurate information.

This is of course the Utopia of e-business for any company, large or small.

Because this technology is so inexpensive and widely available now the small business can act as a very large business and therefore compete globally. The opportunity is phenomenal for those business leaders who have the foresight to reach for it.

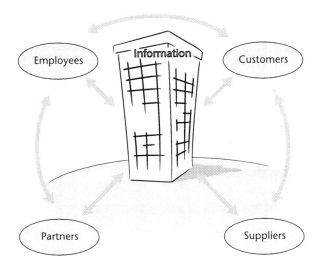

Fig. 5.4

Figure 5.4 shows the future view of any business but the real gains are to be found by those who lead the way. At this very moment, one of your competitors might be reading this book and is about to investigate or even implement a model such as the one shown. How will you compete against them with your manual inefficient and slower approach?

You, the business leader must act quickly.

Find out how your business can embrace the technologies and the e-business models, driving efficiency, speed and flexibility into your business and reaping the benefits of a lower overhead base and greater profits.

PUTTING IT ALL TOGETHER

Hopefully by now, the massive impact of e-business is sharply in focus for you. For those businesses which accept that e-business is the future and not a passing phase, there will be increased profitability and greater market opportunities as their rewards.

For those who shy away from e-business, believing the old world order prevails and that people will always buy from people no matter what the price, then a gradual decline and erosion of their business will be the penalty incurred.

For a small business built to last, the business leader must take sustained action to adopt these new technologies. We say 'sustained' because, on occasions, it will seem difficult to measure the return on your initial investments. In earlier chapters we have told you that the next two years' expectations are always overstated but the next ten are always understated.

Even when it appears that the world is not following you on the technology path, stay with your investment because the world certainly is!

When implementing e-business strategies don't forget the most important principles. Computers and software are simply tools for your business. When deploying these tools ensure that your staff receive exhaustive training as to their use, otherwise you gain only a small fraction of the benefits.

E-business brings about fundamental process changes within any business. As with any major change it may be seen as a threat by your teams, who may in turn not give it the full support that you may require. As well as the training mentioned above, please refer to Chapter 8 *Rapid change management* in order to synchronize with the new business order.

The shape of your e-business solutions will very much depend on the type of business you are. For help or advice in selecting IT partners or suppliers, contact your local Small Business Service, but as with any strategic purchase make absolutely sure that you take up adequate references, see at least three vendors and visit their customers' sites to see the systems working in practice.

When it comes to the support contract, ensure you have more than sufficient training and support built in and don't put pressure on the vendor to deliver five days training in just three.

TECHNICAL INNOVATIONS IN THE NOT-SO-DISTANT FUTURE

Without wishing to confuse you with science, it is worth spending the remainder of this chapter looking at the immediate future in technology terms.

Internet kiosks

It is likely that there will be a sharp increase in the number of customer kiosks in public places such as stores, shopping malls and transport stations.

These kiosks will be based upon delivering Internet-style information for the public user. They are highly likely to be supported by those people who would like to use them for advertising their own companies. Opportunities may arise, for example, if you consider making your services one of those referred to in the kiosk information point, thus reaching out to a new market.

The WAP protocol on telephones

For some time, the WAP phone has been billed as the up-and-coming communications device, but with little evidence to support this. The WAP phone or the wireless application protocol is about delivering cut-down, Internet-based information in the form of text and basic graphics to the screen of a mobile telephone. Via menus you are able to check flight arrival times, bank account information, sports results and your star sign compatibility. It is possible today to check the weather in any number of towns or obtain the telephone number of a local taxi firm in any specific town or city in the UK, simply by entering the abbreviated codes.

New revolutionary personal devices

The WAP protocol on telephones is highly likely to give way to what we term personal devices. A personal device is a wallet-size miniature computer with a large screen with camera, making video conferencing possible, and a permanent connection at high speed to the Internet. This connection costs you nothing, until information is either sent or received.

This personal device will allow immediate e-mail retrieval, more sophisticated and complicated information to be displayed and will undoubtedly have the communication abilities of a telephone, fax machine and answer machine built in.

In time, these devices will combine all the functions of laptop, desktop, computers, phones, organizers, video cameras and any other electronic gadget you can think of! Since these devices will be highly personalized and in constant touch with their base stations, who you are and where you are to within a metre or two will be constantly known to the system. Global positioning satellites could also lock onto your device and pin you down to a few centimetres.

You can even programme your likes and dislikes and when you enter a crowded room, you can automatically find other devices that have similar preference— hence the solution to chat-up lines!

You are probably already targeted by junk advertising e-mails through your previous purchases. In the future, this new consumer purchasing could mean for example, if you want to buy a car, you can buy, finance, specify, and book the test drive using the mobile phone. Having bought it, the mobile device will contact the buyer with ancillary products to purchase.

Infrared devices

The last innovation, which may affect the way we develop our strategies, is code-named 'blue tooth' from IBM. This is the application of intelligent, wireless (infrared or microwave) connected devices. It will be possible for your fridge to contain a blue tooth device, which is cable of scanning the bar code of your pre-packed food as it leaves the fridge. It would then add the same item to your possible shopping list, which you activate over the Internet. Pre-packed food leaves the fridge and the scanned information is passed directly to the microwave which automatically selects the cooking times and settings.

Connected to the above mobile devices, will mean that only the limits of your imagination will constrain the future possibilities.

As business leaders, you must keep yourself informed about developments such as these, as they will have a possible direct bearing upon either your company or your customers. Do not delegate this responsibility to a team operative as the key strategic advantages may be lost in the rush to gain information. As a business leader you may be able to spot the opening or the advantage or indeed a convergence in the market place, but only you will be able to identify this in your business.

It is difficult to establish in a publication such as this, the level of detail which should be conveyed. Clearly every business is different and each market is probably at a different stage in its evolution. In order to continue the e-business discussion we would recommend you contact your local chamber of commerce or Small Business Service, or that you look out for local advertised seminars.

MAKING IT WORK FOR YOUR BUSINESS

For many small businesses there will be no technology expert within the company and the responsibility with fall to the business leader. This difficult situation can often be overcome by the careful use of a well-briefed consultant. The advantage of using external consultants is that they will bring experiences of many e-business projects providing you with the benefit of those experiences.

This experience may short cut your implementation and enhance the possibilities when you take your first steps down the e-business road. As with any consultant, always obtain satisfactory references and take on board the recommendation that if you don't want to accept the consultant's advice, fire them immediately. Don't ever ask a consultant to implement ideas that are either out of their experience zone or not part of their own recommendations.

Whatever form of continuous education you choose, it should also provide you with the opportunity to network with other business leaders and to discover the state of evolution within different sectors and businesses.

Many publications refer to e-business as a revolution, whereas we have described it as evolution. The difference is this. A revolution is a short-lived event of dramatic change, whereas evolution, however dramatic the event is at the outset, is a sustained and never-ending change.

To ensure the success of implementing the new technology within your business, it is important to focus on three key steps:

- understand the technology you have chosen for your business;
- understand its capabilities and benefits to your business;
- create the environment for success.

We have already outlined the first two steps in this chapter, but to be successful in the third step, you will need to ensure commitment from yourself, your team, partners, suppliers and customers. In Chapter 8 *Rapid change management*, we offer a process in which you can action change and innovation into your business with the support from your teams.

Please read this chapter and digest the processes suggested. It will make a great difference to implementing a new, emotive project like IT which affects the entire business in a smooth, controlled manner. Rapid change management (RCM) will assist you in all of your future projects, innovations and future planning activities. See Chapter 6, *Focus on the real customer*, which gives you ideas on how IT can help you identify your true customers and give them what they really want.

It is true to say that one of the reasons business leaders fail to secure the benefits of new technology is that they do not undertake a major rethink of their business processes before application.

It is imperative that the business leader reviews existing processes to see how to reduce inefficiencies with a new, simple operation. This of course can be done through rapid change management techniques or/and with a third party in the form of a consultant.

You have two choices when introducing new technology to your small business:

E-business explosion

- adopt electronic change in line with your existing system, ie parallel the result, or;

- adopt completely new processes to override your existing systems.

Whatever choice you make, ensure that your external relationships as well as your internal ones are taken into account. Suitable links and effective communications to the Internet are therefore paramount to success. Making sure your website is completely customer-friendly and enjoyable to enter should be the end focus criteria to your implementation.

Of course there will be a high level of disruption to your small business as each module or process is installed. You must operate the project with a methodical, step-by-step approach. The whole objective of the new technology is to improve business performance, so you must understand the performance to date.

Review the following aspects of your business,

- What is the current performance?

- What is best practice?

- What benchmarks should you set?

- What new standards do you need to achieve to reach best performance?

- What do your customers, suppliers, partners need from you?

- What is the current performance of your competitors?

The above will guide you to formulate the right decisions and implement the very best processes into your business. With the help of rapid change management, your knowledge and the backing of your team, create the perfect environment to adopt new technologies into your small business built to last.

BUILDING BLOCK 5

- Business to business growth on the Internet is much faster than business to customer on the Internet. However, business to consumer services will increase significantly over the next 10 years.

- The key word for small business is *automation* to increase competitiveness.

- Embrace the technologies and the e-business models. Adopt IT- led changes and connect to all your partners/customers/suppliers where appropriate.

- E-mail will reduce costs and allow your business to adopt a speed that you would never achieve without it.

- As a supplier to your customer, the ability to send electronic notes or attach pictures or complex files within minutes has become a necessity and not a luxury.

- By opening a website on the World Wide Web, your business is automatically international. It can sell and update existing and new customers, link up with suppliers and sell via partners/distributors. All business documents can be accessed remotely away from the office.

- If you shy away from e-business, then a gradual decline and erosion of your business will be seen in the years to follow.

- Challenge the Internet and reach out for the knowledge. It's only a machine connected to a telephone line and you cannot break it.

- Show willingness to be open and to share information with your team, customers, suppliers and partners to truly affect profitability.

- Too much internal focus or too little could create more processes and paperwork and cause impaired performance/few savings.

E-business explosion

6

Focus on the real customer

What makes a good customer?

Tracking the real customer

Use IT to be part of the customer

Creating real customers

The ability to inspire passion, enthusiasm and commitment from employees is an essential quality in developing real customer relationships

WHAT MAKES A GOOD CUSTOMER?

There are many publications in circulation telling us how the customer is king and how we must always try to delight our customers and exceed their expectations. These publications rarely define what it is that makes a customer a good customer as opposed to a poor customer.

Small businesses can spend huge amounts of time attempting to find and keep customers, but rarely differentiate from a desirable customer and just another sales invoice.

Pareto's Law

Pareto's Law states that 80 per cent of the value in your customer base comes from just 20 per cent of the customers. If this is true, why do we spend our time servicing the other 80 per cent?

The answer is, of course, that we rarely understand which 20 per cent provide us with this value!

In our small business that is built to last, it is essential that we understand where our valuable customers are and how we concentrate on finding profitable and therefore valuable new customers.

Let us examine some of the things that make a customer valuable or not.

Attributes of a poor value customer may be:

- they always buy on price;
- they expect pre-sales advice for free;
- they may expect or ask for 'deal sweeteners' or give-aways that enhance your proposal;
- they pay you when they feel like it;
- they treat you as a supplier who is a commodity;
- they never allow you access to senior or board level management;
- they expect your corporate hospitality and their christmas card invites you to buy them a drink each year!

On the other hand, attributes from a valuable customer might be:

- they treat you as a partner within their business;
- they share strategic plans with you;
- they are as much concerned with your support ability tomorrow as they are with your price today;
- they will often pay for pre-sales consultancy;
- they always settle invoices in a reasonable time;
- they will often enter into rental or retainer contracts and look for innovative deal arrangements.

In the first scenario, your business will experience increased overhead charges to support the client for nothing while being forced to reduce your pricing to compete or to win the deal. There is little loyalty from this type of customer and certainly no partnership.

This type of customer may turn into a 'one-off deal' and there is certainly no guarantee of a next deal.

The second scenario suggests a customer who shares the opportunities and the risks and looks for profitable partnerships, which last over time and therefore reduces the overhead of constantly having to find new suppliers.

It is these types of customers we find as valuable, as for the small business, the ability to sell to an existing customer is far less expensive than the operation to find a new customer. Therefore the profitability of the second deal onwards is extremely high.

focus on the real customer

This is clearly the type of customer that any small business would wish to have and if we are to build a business to last then this is the real customer.

We are now going to suggest that you perform an exercise, which unfortunately exposes your information systems as being less than adequate. The exercise is simply to measure the profitability in financial terms and then, albeit subjectively, in real terms.

Test of profitability

The test of profitability in financial terms would be to plot the turnover of all the deals performed with each customer. Now examine the gross margin in percentage and real terms. Next, attribute a level of resource to this customer overall, which takes into account the amount of free pre-sales work, corporate entertainment and other costs associated such as the number of visits to secure the deal, etc.

Once this exercise has been completed, you should know which of your customers are valuable and the answers may surprise you. For what we believe to be our best customers are sometimes our poorest customers in real terms.

As we said earlier, this exercise may be difficult for you to perform as small business rarely maintains information as detailed as this. The following pages look at the effective use of IT to create automated management information systems (MIS) in order for you to perform instant analysis in the future.

TRACKING THE REAL CUSTOMER

Let us ask you a series of questions:

1 How many telephone calls do you receive into your business?
2 Which customers call you and when?
3 How many calls does your business make to customers?
4 What is the content of each discussion?

5 Do you have a process for holding information about a customer?

6 Can you produce reports on all of the above automatically?

7 Are these information systems available to all your team?

8 Do they link to your accounts function?

For many small businesses it starts with a simple database. For a few hundred pounds, a slightly more sophisticated database such as Maximiser, ACT, or Goldmine can be purchased, which allows you to log incoming calls, information received and documents sent against a single customer entry.

For many, the use of these systems extends to about 25 per cent of its capabilities. Hardly anybody logs each call received and documents are rarely linked to the contact details. For the small business built to last, this has to change. Your semi-automated systems are the key to retaining real customers and this has to be communicated throughout your business.

It is worth the investment, not just purchasing the software but also purchasing the time of a qualified installation consultant who can tailor the database fields to your business, connect the database to your office systems, and link to your accounts package. This is a single investment, which will return profitability to you many times over in the future.

Steps to consider during the installation are as follows.

- Every team member existing and new, must be fully trained in the use of this system.

- Set key objectives surrounding the maintenance of accurate information about real customers.

- Back these systems up daily and hold this information as a jewel of your business.

- Ensure security is sufficient such that unauthorized copying or unauthorized access is strictly controlled.

- If you run remote offices such as individual sales people, for example, it is possible for you to provide, either on laptops or home PCs, a small subset of your corporate database relating to their own sales prospects only. This allows you to retain central control over the corporate database, while allowing your remote workers to use the same systems. Their subset and your corporate database are synchronized over the telephone line as often as you wish. This ensures that the corporate database is maintained and updated.

The idea is that every contact conversation, attempted contact and copies of all information, given or sent, are recorded in limitless free text detail against the customer record. Key permanent information is recorded in pre-defined fields, which are visible every time you access this customer record. For example, telephone number, address, number of employees, market sector, key contact individuals are all held in defined fields.

Many contact database packages allow you to set a contact alarm against customer information, where an alarm screen pops up on the defined date at the required time to prompt you to contact your customer. This type of semi-automated process is invaluable in small business, as it alleviates the needs for a fallible human to remember everything.

The term 'customer relationship management' (CRM) is larger businesses quest to personalize information at the point of contact. Large companies spend huge sums of money trying to make the customer feel special by personalizing their value proposition. This can be easily discovered in the home shopping catalogues, who hold personalized information, about you, your family, your credit rating, and your historic purchases. This information is brought up in seconds to the call handler who can access your enquiry and personalize the response immediately. This puts the customer at ease with the sales process, reduces time wastage and encourages the repeat buying cycle.

While contact software such as that described above goes a long way towards holding such personalized information, you may like to consider additional ways of offering an individual value proposition to each customer. This can be done by holding information about the customer's current business set-up or the current use of your product and the problems that it solves.

In our computer services company, we used our customer databases to hold information about our customers' existing computer installations. We were therefore able to configure our solutions to automatically fit into their existing hardware and remove any doubts the customer might have had about configuration. By personalizing our offer in this way, we were seen to have a good understanding of our customers' business, which was difficult for our competitors to replicate.

Data Protection Act

The Data Protection Act 1984, subsequently amended in 1998, requires businesses that store 'personal' data to register with the Data Protection Registrar.

A form is available from the UK Post Office or Small Business Service and a small registration fee may be payable.

The information that you must declare is defined as 'data relating to living people, who may be identified by the information held'. A sole trader is also classified as a living person but a limited company is not.

There are eight internationally agreed principles on data protection. Data must be:

- accurate and up to date;
- used for the purpose for which it is registered;
- obtained legally;
- disclosed as specified at the time of registration;
- relevant to the purpose;
- made available to the person described by the data upon written request;
- removed from records when the data has served its purpose;
- protected by the holder against loss or disclosure.

Generally speaking, every business must assess its obligation to register under the Data Protection Act whether this information is held in computer systems or in manual records.

Exclusions to the Data Protection Act are as follows:

- personal family or household data where the storage of this information is only available to the individuals;
- mailing lists of names and addresses (except where supplementary information such as historic purchases are listed);

- information held for national security purposes;
- information on employee pensions;
- company payrolls.

Buying a database

At some point in time, your small business will require new customers and new prospects. Using sources such as Dunn and Bradstreet, it is possible to buy a computer database of names, addresses and telephone numbers, which is deemed to be up to date and relevant to your criteria. You could for example, order for a few hundred pounds, a list of 10,000 businesses with a turnover of more than £5 million and more than 200 employees in the household, goods and textile markets based in the London and Home Countries area.

By carefully importing this information into your database as above, then you are able to market against defined and qualified customers.

What your criteria should be will obviously depend upon your product, service, market sector, price point and geographical coverage, among other things.

For more information regarding agencies that offer these databases for sale, contact your local Small Business Service.

In your small business built to last, having found a customer of value, you can follow the same value proposition and contact other potential customers in the same market sector. For example, if you had some success selling to a large retailer, it would be fairly obvious to purchase a small database of other major retailers and to take a similar proposition to them. The real costs of this exercise would reduce significantly due to the expertise gained from the first sales win. Expertise within your company, with respect to a certain type of customer or indeed to previous experiences, should be explored as this may allow you to purchase database information for market segments in which you have more knowledge than others.

For more information about this, see Chapter 9 *Driving sales*.

USE IT TO BE PART OF THE CUSTOMER

In the section above our small business built to last has adopted and implemented a simple but sophisticated method of tracking customer contact and sales winning process. This will allow us in future months and years, to analyze profitable customers, track buying patterns and spot the real customers emerging within our business, allowing us to focus our efforts of building long-term partnerships with them.

The use of e-mail to communicate with customers is well known for many small businesses. It allows us to break down any barriers that exist to stop us from communicating directly with the right people.

It has the added benefit of allowing the customer to create internal teams, which can also include you, by virtue of your e-mail inclusion. For example, if a customer starts a project that may involve your company supplying goods or services, how great would it be for you to receive copies of all the internal, project-focused e-mails from your customer's company?

You will be seen as part of the project team. Your costs of doing business with this customer will plummet as e-mail can be far more efficient than physical meetings or letters.

Before we congratulate ourselves on the use of e-mail be very clear about four points:

1. The tone of an e-mail lies somewhere between a formal memo, a telephone call and a personal letter. Over time, e-mails can become very informal and the business leader must ensure that protocol exists within the team for such communications.
2. As your customer becomes a real customer and turns into a partner, familiarity will become the norm. It is essential that the line is not overstepped by copying flippant content, jokes or other fun applications to the client. This is a simple way of eroding the trust between your and your customer.
3. The use of the copy function and reply all within e-mail, means that you can circulate your reply or the information received to many individuals or groups of individuals within seconds. If we

focus on the real customer

had a pound for every incorrect, inappropriate or simply mistaken copy of e-mails sent then we would have retired years ago. Be very careful when handling e-mail to and from your clients, as very often, previously written text is tagged to your e-mail and a conversation that was an 'internal only' e-mail finds itself on a key decision-maker's desk.

4   On a final legal point, you may well have noticed that some e-mails arrive at your desk with an impressive footnote declaring your legal responsibilities to maintain confidentiality, delete after use, etc. For all the reasons mentioned above, it is essential that you implement such a footnote in your business too. The simplest way of doing this is to ask a solicitor to send you a test e-mail and cut and past their footnote into your own!

Taking these precautions enables you at least to have the legal argument if problems arise, or losses result as a consequence of anything you put in an e-mail.

The use of e-mail to communicate to your customers will inevitably lead to your sending information such as word processor documents or spreadsheet information. Before you do this, however, it is worth establishing what systems and version levels your customer is able to use. There is little point sending a Word 2000 file to an Office 1997 user, as they may not be able to access your document. You can, however, save your Word 2000 file in a lower version file, to allow your customer to have access. Simple things like this will save you time and allow your client to build a stronger relationship with your business.

In the earlier sections we mentioned that a real customer will form a partnership and allow you an insight into their business strategies and contact with their senior management. If you are always the recipient of information it makes for a fairly one-sided conversation. So how do we get regular and up-to-date information about our real customers, their markets and the factors affecting them as businesses?

It is possible to do this manually but this is not desirable, as it means substantial ongoing research. By using the Internet, it is possible to accept daily e-mails from various sources relevant to our real customers, for example:

- taking e-mails from industry sector news groups;
- e-mails from the stock exchange for your real customers' share price;
- sectoral analysis by using a portal to your customers' market place.

Taking this information in electronic form makes it two clicks away from sharing it with your entire team and other interested parties. IT can be used effectively in your business at almost no cost to provide complex and up-to-date information to support your relationship with the real customer.

For more information on setting up news feeds and e-mail feeds, visit your Small Business Service or employ the services of a qualified consultant who is able to do this for you, and more importantly train you to do it yourself.

CREATING REAL CUSTOMERS

So far in this chapter, we have looked at the enormously positive effects of concentrating on your real customers and the substantially higher profits to be made by this focus. We then examined the IT infrastructure required to record and measure information about all of our customers. Finally, we looked at the supporting technologies that allow you to add significant but inexpensive value to your customers.

> *If we were to define the ideal customer, it might be a business that doesn't necessarily buy on price, buys regularly, and doesn't go to competing suppliers. If your business had a number of such customers, which enabled you to plot your future monthly sales accurately, and demonstrate profits into the future, what a valued business you would have.*

This concept is often used by venture capitalists or other investors to determine the predictability or sustainability of the business. The small business built to last must attempt to convert its customers into those described above. How?

Locking the customer into your business

Each small business will have a different set of criteria and opportunities in its operation. *Therefore, the criteria and opportunities will operate over large market sectors so the strategies outlined below are general in their description, but when fine-tuned for your market will deliver the results.* The strategies are:

- finding quality repeat earnings;
- use of financial tools;
- increase your order value.

■ Finding quality repeat earnings

The term 'repeat earnings' often refers to a rental contract, a maintenance agreement payment or a regular customer invoice for such things as consumables. Therefore the supplier of straws to Macdonald's may have a forward contract order for the supply of these consumables, which stretches out to the months ahead.

A photocopier supplier may also derive monthly income by the use of a rental contract for toner or paper purchase, which are deemed high turnover consumables.

These types of business are able to plan the future with a far greater degree of certainty than for those of us who start from zero from the sales board each month. Building a business to last means that we are going to have to seek out repeat earnings potential from all of our clients in order to cushion our business against sales downturns.

If you don't have a product and you are selling service, identify methods of adjusting your charging structures to allow for a retainer. As a consultant, for example, asking the customer to pay a small monthly retainer, which would give them the benefit of either free telephone advice or a lower charge rate when you attended site, may be a way of introducing repeat earnings to your business.

> *Tip: Think long and hard about different ways in which you can charge for your service or goods in such a way that you are able to take regular income from your customers.*

For some small businesses, you may argue that you simply sell capital goods with one-off payments from the customer. If this is the case consider the use of financial tools as discussed below. The net effect of repeat earnings is to establish a regular presence with your customer allowing them to consider you as a partner and not simply a single supplier.

It will also justify in your own mind your desire to spend more time working with the customer identifying new sales opportunities.

■ Use of financial tools

For those business leaders who are not comfortable with talking finance, then we strongly advise you to take some time out and accept training or read a practical finance book relating to small businesses. Try the *Small Business Handbook* (Webb and Webb, Prentice Hall, 2001), which also includes a CD-ROM containing financial worksheets for you to have and use.

For many large businesses where capital purchase budgets may not be readily available, the use of financial tools such as lease or rental agreements may be just the factor that wins the deal.

If you are selling to smaller businesses they will probably welcome this offer from you, as they too may wish to protect their available cash and be prepared to pay for your goods on a monthly or quarterly basis. Of course the last thing your small business needs is to offer your customers a small monthly sum opposed to the larger real cost of the service or equipment. This is where a finance company enters the scene.

Every industry sector has preferred finance companies operating within that sector. Some operate for business levels only above and about £100,000, while others go down to amounts as low as £2,000. The idea is simple. The finance house agrees to enter into a triangulated agreement between your business, themselves and your customer. You are able to present this offering as your own company in conjunction with, or backed by, the finance house. Your customers, assuming the credit check passes, are able to accept a rental plan or lease over an agreed time period for exchange for your goods or services.

The main advantages to your customers are:

■ they can spread their payments over say three years;
■ they enjoy the benefits of the service immediately.

Your customer is obligated to make payments to, say, three years, during which time they are not permitted to make any changes, add-ons, disposals, etc without your prior written acceptance. They are in effect locked in to your business.

Of course there are ways around this, but these would incur significant time and effort. Your business on the other hand benefits tremendously.

- Between 7–10 days of the issuing of the invoice for the goods and services, the finance company pays you the gross amount less the interest charges over the time period.
- This is a massive cash boost for your business, which is recovered in full in about a quarter of the time that it takes your best customers to pay their 30-day invoices.
- You have achieved the next best thing to a quality repeat earning.

If it is relevant, always credit clear your client for more money than they need for your initial order. In this way, you can sell further goods and services to the customer, who then simply has to authorize a fractional increase in their monthly or quarterly payments. Again your gross payment will be returned to you, 7–10 days after you submit your second invoice.

As you may have gathered by now, if your products require maintenance or licence fees to be paid annually, then you will be submitting these invoices upfront to cover the finance period.

You are in effect charging capital sum plus licence plus maintenance for the next three years within one single invoice, payable in full by the finance company 7–10 days later.

When you engage a finance company on this basis, ensure they are comfortable with:

- your product/service (as some fund non-capital goods);
- the triangular agreement;
- not offering personal guarantees.

Try to select a finance company from your market sector, as they may be able to offer a better deal based on familiarity with your product.

As a test, ask them to credit check a selection of your current customer base to ensure a fit. This has the obvious benefit of credit clearing your customers or prospects before you have the financial discussion.

When discussing the financier's various products, be aware that some offer flexible payment plans, which can provide your customers with lower initial payments, no payments for the next three months or lower overall payments with what is called a balloon or final payment at the end.

Make sure that these are explained adequately to you, and if you don't understand, ask them to explain it to you again.

For information about where you can find suitable finance partners, refer to your local Small Business Service, chamber of commerce, bank manager, accountant, your industry sector periodical/newspaper or membership organization.

■ Increase your order value

The most expensive activity a small business undertakes is finding a new customer. Assuming that you have secured that customer by winning that order and you are firmly convinced that this is a real customer, then let us look at extracting the maximum value from this relationship.

In the section above we have looked at using financial tools to be able to use a finance company for charges and support contracts over the term of the customer's agreement. In much the same way, we are going to examine the principal of increasing each order value with your customers. Let us illustrate how you can do this with an example.

> **Example:** If you sold an item for £100 it costs you £50 in real terms to win the order and your relative overheads were always 30 per cent of the order value, then we can see that the total profit for this new customer is £100 less £50 sell cost, less 30 per cent administration (£30) which leads £20 net profit.
>
> *If, in the same selling meeting* you were to increase this order value to £140, then the sell cost would still be £50, the overheads would be 30 per cent (£52) leaving a net profit of £38.

focus on the real customer

In this example, by increasing the sales order value by 40 per cent to £140, the net profit on this same deal rose from £20 to £38, which is an increase of 90 per cent.

Therefore, by increasing each order value wherever possible, we achieve a disproportionately larger increase in the net profits.

So how do we do this?

If you go down to your local market, you are sure to find the man with the towels. You will never succeed in buying a single towel from this trader, as he only ever sells in value packs or unbelievable bargains!

While we are not suggesting that you say to your customer, 'have I got a deal for you', we are suggesting that you examine how your business can bundle products or services together in order to achieve a higher gross sale.

Be imaginative in your pricing methods, as your selling costs for the second bundled item in the same sales meeting is zero!

You can afford to be generous and innovative in the way that you bundle products or services by referring to the method above.

By adopting this technique, we believe that you can run increase in turnover and increase in profit simultaneously, putting aside the old saying 'turnover is vanity and profit is sanity'.

For more information about driving sales, see Chapter 9 *Driving sales*.

In this chapter we have taken time to build our knowledge and experience to identify, measure and form partnerships with real customers as opposed to sales contacts who buy from us on price, and discard us as commodity suppliers. We now have a set of tools and strategies, which will allow us to build a high-quality customer base to be serviced by our small business for many years to come. For it is only to focus on the real customer that we are able to survive in business and ensure that our small business is built to last.

BUILDING BLOCK 6

- Remember that 80 per cent of the value in your customer base comes from just 20 per cent of the customers.

- The ability to sell to an existing customer is far less expensive than the operation to find a new one.

- Hold information on all of your customers to find your real customers.

- Use IT to be part of your customer's operation.

- Understand your good customers and lock them into your business.

- Seek out repeat earnings potential from your customers.

- Offer varied finance tools to your customers.

- Increase your order value by examining how you bundle products or services together.

- Form partnerships with your real customers.

- Share strategic plans with your customer.

focus on the real customer

7

Picking your partners – cultivating your allies

How do you select the right partner(s)?

Assistance in finding the right partner

Formulating the relationship with a market vision

Key measurements

Systems connect

Syndication

Acquistions

In today's fiercely competitive global market place, small businesses can no longer compete by effort alone. Alliances are the way forward to achieve sustained competitive edge

For larger businesses, we often hear about partnerships being formed, which add value in the market place and therefore supports the share price of the businesses concerned.

In larger organizations, teams of strategists spend a great deal of time identifying the negotiating parameters, drawing up businesses plans and working out delivery plans, etc.

For our small businesses, we simply just don't have this time or resource available to us.

So how do small businesses find out about commercial partners that add value to our businesses and provide us with a foundation for the future as opposed to being a costly distraction?

For most business leaders, the opportunity to form a partnership stems from commonality with a single customer, or from personal contacts in the business leaders' network forums. There may be more willingness than synergy in the early stages and most partnerships based on this may not last.

If a small business puts enough time and effort into identifying key partners and allies, then the rewards are certainly worth having. Some of the key advantages to working with partners in the market place instead of alone include the following.

- The partner's sales force can be considered as an extension of your own.
- Joint marketing initiatives cover more ground for less cost.
- Customer bases of both businesses can be farmed for joint reward.

- The number of key customer reference sites will expand.
- You may be able to access different markets through your partner.
- Your product sets delivered together maybe greater than the two halves.
- A joint learning process starts resulting in shared resource, systems and occasionally people.

HOW DO YOU SELECT THE RIGHT PARTNER(S)?

It is important that you identify the different types of partner available to your business. They fall into two broad categories:

- those who resell your product;
- those who introduce you directly to the customer.

Those partners who resell your product or service may be distributors, resellers, consultancy companies or commercial companies.

Those partners who introduce you to their clients may be commercial organizations with different product sets, selling agents or signposting organizations, such as the Small Business Service, for example.

> *There may be a strategic reason why you would wish to select a certain specific partner in a market. It relates to your strategic business plan and your desire to expand your business by acquisition.*

What better way then to qualify the acquisition by turning them into a proven, trusted partner? The last section of this chapter describes the acquisition process in detail.

Product analysis

Before you select the right partner, it is essential for you to test the ability of your product or service to be delivered via a partner. This will narrow down your selection process.

- For example, if your company sells a product which is manufactured by yourself and requires little selling activity per product,

picking your partners – cultivating your allies

then your partnership search is likely to start with a distributor or reseller.

- If your products or services are less tangible and require significant selling activity, then you are likely to find introduction partners more beneficial.

- If however, your company sells products manufactured by others, then selecting a commercial partner with synergistic products may provide the best working partnership.

Regardless of the route that may or not be apparent to you at this time, the next question is one of pricing strategy. Most partnerships work on the basis of either shared revenue or commissions paid.

Examine the customer price and the real cost to your business. If your product is to be sold via a reseller then you have to be able to offer a meaningful percentage discount, which will act as their profit margin. This is usually between 25–40 per cent, depending on the market sector. If you offer any less than this amount, you will not gain the continual attention of your partner's sales team, which will be a false saving over time.

Selection by geographic coverage

An easy selection criterion is to address geographic presence. If your business is regionalized for whatever reason, then finding a partner in a different region will add value to the business.

A last point to geographic presence is the possibility of an overseas appointment, which will give you access to non-English-speaking markets. If you do this, however, you must be prepared to translate your support documentation into other languages, adopting any other legislative or functional requirements of that market.

Reaching unobtainable customers

For many small businesses, especially those built to last, real customers of a larger nature are often more difficult to close. The reasons are straightforward in that they are usually very big and you are usually small. They have professional processes in place and you may take a less formal approach. Of course your financial strength as a business may cause them to question their logic in placing a large order representing a high percentage of your company's turnover.

So, we seek partners in order to deliver to these larger real customers. The type of partners that we seek at this point, are much bigger than our own company and will already have a close selling relationship with our intended customer.

If they have this relationship it is likely to be a specialized supply relationship with products similar but not the same as our own. A typical example can be found in the computer industry where EDS and CSC supply computer solutions to large blue chip clients. As a small business if we could convince EDS or CSC to take on our product then we would be able to have conversations, via their sales force, with multiple blue-chip real customers.

Clearly these partnerships are not formed overnight, and will require a selling process in itself to be applied over time.

The advantages of such a relationship are abundantly clear. Through these system integrator partners, it will be possible for a smaller business to sell its products and services to multiple blue chip organizations without the associated costs with direct selling to companies of this size.

This type of partnership is two way in as far as the indicator would make a profit margin on your product and gain additional consultancy revenue by implementing into their corporate accounts. Your business on the other hand would benefit from a surge in revenue, and the ability to site large blue chip clients among your users.

A word of caution, however, as by selling indirectly to these blue chip customers, it is not possible to hold the customer relationship and therefore your true customer who is in this case, your partner. Be clear that your strategy here, is for revenue growth and not direct customer contact.

Value add products

The last selection criterion we are going to offer in this section is the prospect of finding a partner who sells products which add value to your own. These products should be of a similar value to the customer, both in terms of functionality as well as price. Why?

- There is no point asking a partner company to sell your £10,000 products when the cost of their own product is only £1,000.
- Their sales force will feel unqualified to make this substantially larger sale and will not have the confidence to take it into their customers.
- There is also no point in asking a partner to sell your valuable solution when they are in the business of price-sensitive commodity.

A good way of spotting other product vendors is to simply ask your customer. Your customers will tell you which suppliers they might like you to get closer to and will benefit from their suppliers collaborating for mutual gain.

In the sections above, we have suggested criteria by which you would like to select your partners, at this stage, you may not know the name of your partner but understand the size and shape you would like them to be.

ASSISTANCE IN FINDING THE RIGHT PARTNER

The local government office in each of the regions may assist you in identifying partnerships and may be able to help you search out the names of companies you can approach.

Alternatively, look to your trade journals, exhibitions, seminar activity and customer referrals as your points of enquiry.

Examine the financial position of prospective partners and look at their websites in detail to confirm their suitability.

It is now up to you, as the business leader to seek a meeting with the directors of this company and explore the synergies and mutual understanding. Despite all the hard work to date, this is the time to rely on your feelings as to the cultural fit, dedication to the customer and enthusiasm that comes across.

Test it thoroughly and if you have any doubts whatever, conclude the meeting and move on.

Tip: *Remember, more partnerships in small businesses fail than succeed.*

A partnership for a small business is like a marriage. Consider it so when you form it. Give it time and attention and if the feeling is reciprocated, then the chances of succeeding will go up. Don't settle for second best and don't be disheartened if your initial search process or indeed your first partner selection turns out badly.

Tip: *Partners, when chosen correctly, will add substantial value to your small business, and you must persevere in your quest.*

FORMULATING THE RELATIONSHIP WITH A MARKET VISION

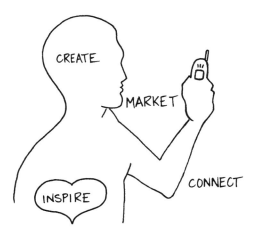

Innovation is the key to improve business performance. Research by Living Innovation shows how, through a commitment to innovation, companies can outperform their competitors, introduce new and exciting products and services, in order to meet and then exceed market expectations.

For the purpose of this section we are going to assume that you have found a partner with whom you wish to work. This partner is likely to be larger than yourself, and therefore have an existing brand presence in the market.

picking your partners – cultivating your allies

Brand extension is one of the most powerful endorsing methods in today's commercial world. When IBM, for example, adopts a software package from a smaller supplier, the kudos associated with buying IBM products is automatically associated with the lesser-known application.

Branded endorsement could be a most powerful message to the market, especially where your customers are very much bigger than you are. If a large customer agrees to act as a reference site for your products and services, this sends a strong message to prospective customers who are about to buy from you. It says, if this large branded customer has bought and succeeded with this smaller business, then I will be able to as well. The brand and size of the reference account carries you on to another sale, but in the world of brand extension, an official endorsement without usage will be just as effective.

Think about your large suppliers and customers, and see if you can attract written statements of endorsement from them. Similarly, if your products form a part of a well-known company's product than brand extension will occur and you will benefit.

One of the first areas of activity you will agree when forming partnerships is to perform some type of marketing activity to an agreed number of customers to announce your partnership.

- This may take many forms but collaborative mail shots or seminar activities are often effective first steps.
- Establish early on the basis for cost allocation in all marketing activities, as this may well advantage you by providing piggy-back access to a much larger marketing fund.
- Take every opportunity to market your products, or indeed your joining products internally, to both your sales force and that of your partners.
- Make sure you communicate properly your vision and your values for both your products and your intended market.

These are intangible but necessary aspects of marketing within a partnership. When the relationship is more established, it will surely be possible to plan out other marketing activity such as speculative seminars and organized exhibitions. Stand sharing at an exhibition can provide you with access to marketing opportunities that were previously out of your reach. Imagine your company for example, exhibiting in Earls Court or Hanover in Germany, as part of one of the major trade fairs which most serious buyers attend.

If you are operating a distributor model for your product, make your marketing information available to your distributor, which at their own cost, they can customize with their own contact details, pricing, etc.

Where a distributor wishes to undertake specific marketing activities to sell your products, you must be prepared to support them in real terms. It is often common that a distributor will accrue a penny of every pound's worth of products that they sell. This accrual is held as a marketing fund which if your distributor cares to match, pound for pound, you can release what we call co-operative marketing, on an agreed case-by-case basis.

There may be occasions when a partnership is proven, where you may consider a secondment of staff in either direction in order to demonstrate commitment and remove any barriers to the selling or cross-selling of products or services.

Good partnerships, when operated well can afford a small business a high-quality repeat earnings channel. They can deliver turnover and market presence quickly and efficiently to the small business that strives to be built to last.

KEY MEASUREMENTS

As with any new project, key milestones and measurements must be agreed with your partner beforehand. It is essential that you are able to measure independently from each other:

- the amount of marketing;
- its cost;
- the resultant enquiries;
- moving to a measurement of the sales enquiries to proposal ratio;
- then from proposals to close ratios.

See Chapter 9 *Driving sales* for further information.

We have so often seen medium-sized businesses that build up many reselling partners in the early years with no real understanding of the profitability of the relationship. Subsequently, the new director who has just joined this company, takes measurements, assesses each partnership and terminates 90 per cent of them. These directors are considered to be successful, simply because they have stripped costs and unproductive effort out of their companies.

Try to avoid the mistake of appointing 20 partners in the hope that one might come good for you. It is far better to build a series of qualified partners, adding value to your business in different areas, different ways and in different geographies.

The question we always ask when assessing the effectiveness of a partnership is 'have we invoiced a real customer yet?' Don't lose sight of the goal in all of this joint marketing activity and convergence of cultures. The end result must provide a customer who can be invoiced.

It is quite usual for the first customer to be identified and pursued by you the business leader and a senior level executive within your partner's organization. Once the lesson has been learnt and success demonstrated, then it is time to educate your sales team and move your role to that of manager and measurer.

SYSTEMS CONNECT

As in previous sections where we have discussed the advantages of using IT infrastructure to enhance the relationship with your customer, we are going to explore some of the ways where this infrastructure can be extended to your partners and even to your suppliers.

In any collaborative venture or new partnership, the first idea that a company has is to put out a press statement. This is actually more to do with making a public statement about the director's intentions as opposed to attracting new customers. This joint press release can often be a point at which the two marketing systems come together. In some cases unfortunately it is the last.

If we are to form truly effective partnerships then we have to be prepared to connect our systems as well as our intentions. Historically this has led to a large amount of manual process, cost and in some cases disruption to the individual businesses.

Information technology, particularly the Internet, makes collaborative systems far easier to implement than ever before. For more proactive businesses the website is in fact part of their press office and so the press announcement described earlier will appear in the website newsroom. The website is the ideal medium for the further convergence of systems as they are so easy and inexpensive to change and add information to. Therefore your products can be written into the product sheets of your partner's website within hours for very little cost.

If the relationship is more arm's length, then by providing a simpler link button, commonly known as a hyper link, that sits either on a partner's page, the home page or part of the press release, users of your partner's website will be able to hop to your website at a click of a mouse. *This system of hyper-linking is known as 'affinity links'.*

The respective websites can be used and updated regularly to reflect joint sales wins, combined product bundles, and joint seminar or exhibition activity. Don't forget you are in control of your own website, so if things don't work out, you can simply delete all references within minutes.

The website is only the beginning. By making pages of information available to your partners, that for example, they can only see using security pass words, then you offer them the ability to download whole documents or brochures electronically. The advantage of offering this is that they are able to control the information flow to their customers and provide on-demand information relating to your products or services.

If this were to become a regular requirement you may consider setting up an *extranet* to exist between you and your partners. (An extranet is a secure environment where specific information is made available via your company's intranet; see Chapter 5 *E-business explosion* for a reminder of these terms.)

For a very small outlay now, you have created a partner forum whereby interactive and collaborative working can take place. Let us not forget the obvious e-mail possibilities with your small business e-mails being

picking your partners – cultivating your allies

transferred to the corporate address books of your partners, and indeed vice versa.

As suggested, with your customers, this will break down some of the barriers, allowing informal e-mail communications to take over for a more formal telephone call, letter or proposal.

> *When you consider making these steps, please ensure that you have adequate virus protection and system security in place.*

There is nothing worse than exposing a valuable partner to a malicious virus or a breach of security that could have been so easily avoided. Small companies are not always to blame for these indiscretions, as we have known many large companies from which viruses have been transmitted.

In matters of partnership systems, the Internet, being the low cost and flexible medium that it is offers you inexpensive yet sophisticated tools to bind your partners to your business. Websites operate 24 hours a day, 7 days per week and e-mail knows no time zones.

SYNDICATION

As a final point to the section on partnerships and allies, we would like to describe an emerging trend relating to the use of the Internet and embracing the concept of partnerships using information. Syndication can be described as follows:

A syndicate is an association of people or companies formed to engage in an enterprise or promote a common interest.

Therefore:

Syndication of a product or service means that it becomes distributable through this partner association to multiple outlets.

This currently happens in a variety of traditional media forms, with production, music and radio studios, journalists and photographers selling their products to multiple outlets: different TV and radio networks, newspapers and magazines.

Three key points demonstrate the Internet's place as the perfect medium for syndication:

1 **Information is all**. Syndication fits information goods like a glove. The lifeblood of the Internet is information.

2 **Modularity**. Optimum performance of syndication increases exponentially with the level of modularity of the product.

3 **Recycling**. Digital information is the ultimate recyclable product. The Internet provides countless distribution points, which means information can be recycled endlessly, creating multiple revenue opportunities. Not only can a high-demand product such as the Madonna live concert be broadcast through numerous outlets, the archive can also be accessed an infinite number of times by paying consumers.

The gradual transformation of the Internet from its perceived chaotic state to a more structured entity involves an essential mindset change that wholly embraces a new way of looking at business and information management. It involves the transfer of syndication into a viable format for the virtual world.

Syndication applies to information being placed into a common entity by many partners for the purpose of deriving benefit from this combination. Remember that this could equally apply to information about physical products. So whatever business you are in, think about syndication as a route to a common goal.

ACQUISTIONS

Your strategy to identify market acquisitions may have been a driver for your selecting a given company as a partner. Statistics show the huge difficulties of integrating acquired firms into the purchasing company and the many disappointments that are evident in cultural mismatch or misunderstandings.

In order for your acquisition to be successful you may have decided that to partner the identified company, joint market with them, achieve sales together and share systems, was an ideal way to reduce the risks as stated above.

The major steps that will take place are as follows.

1 Draw up Head of Agreement between all shareholders.

2 Inform your accountant of choice, which may not be your retained accountant.

3 Inform the appointed solicitor who will act for you. Ensure that the firm has experience in this type of work, and references that you can take up for your market sector and the size of company that you are.

4 Be prepared to spend considerable time at a senior level, in order to perform checks and due diligence.

5 The process of direct meetings can now take place in order to ascertain the potential match between the two businesses. Various discussions can take place about the structure of a deal, the amounts payable, the timescales, etc.

6 If you can agree a deal, the legal process can start to roll, and usually takes around three months to complete.

The first order of business, then, is to appoint a firm of solicitors to represent you in the process of purchase. This is clearly a vital decision, one that you must take steadily, and after having met and interviewed three or four possible companies.

Ask them how they would approach the purchase, and ask for three references. Don't be hesitant in requesting these references, as the information given to you may well influence the appointment in what is the most critical decision of your business life to date.

From the moment that you appoint solicitors and instruct the acquisition, your business enters a time of uncertainty.

Valuation of the business you wish to acquire

Factors that will be considered when the valuation is performed include the following.

- How long have they been in business?
- What market place do they sell into?
- Are they in control of their market place?

- Do they sell something that is unique or do they add value in a unique way?

- Does their business attract 'quality earnings'? These may be long-term customer contracts, royalties, leasing commissions, licence fees to the customer base, and guaranteed earnings of other sorts.

- Who are their customers, and are these customers desirable (blue chip, for instance)?

- What level of sales do they have?

- What is their underlying profitability?

- What is their net asset position?

- Do they have an attractive future in an expanding market?

- Are they people based, or product based for success?

- Does their business rely upon an individual in order to be successful, or do they have a strong management team that runs the daily business?

There are probably other factors that you will consider with advice from your solicitors.

The price earnings multiple

There is one other term that you need to understand in the pricing of a business, and that is 'price earnings multiple'.

If you take their average net profits, assuming that they are relatively consistent over the last few years, and deduct tax at the appropriate rate, you will end up with a net after tax figure. The price earnings multiple (PEM or PE ratio) is a number between 1 and, say, 30, which the market place will support as the company's value. If you look in the *Financial Times*, the right-hand column will tell you what the PE is for each company listed.

In the engineering sector, for example, a factor on average of 17 may be expected, whereas the biotech sector, which is generally thought to be very high growth, can carry a PE of anything from 20 to 50. These figures are for public quoted companies of a certain size and position in the market. For a small private business in an average sector, with a few years' trading and average profits, the PEM is usually around 4–9.

picking your partners – cultivating your allies

Example: A light engineering consultancy, employing 15 people, with turnover of £750,000 to 20 or so blue chip companies, producing a profit of about £70,000 each year. The market is static, and there is no formal management team in place. The business has forward contracts of three months' worth of work, and relies upon the staff employed to maintain the relationships with the clients. The business has been trading at this level for about four years, and has a net asset position of £250,000. The business is considered to be competent and leading the way in solution provision to engineering problems.

The prospective purchaser should appraise the business as follows:

- management is weak, but this is not too much of a problem as long as the staff stay in place and the customers transfer;
- the 20 customers are a good spread;
- the customers are blue chip and can probably be developed for greater return;
- forward contracts are fine, but the purchaser should consider what happens next?
- the engineering sector is not in great shape right now, so there is a risk of revenue reduction in the coming year;
- the £70,000 profit is fair by percentage, and there is a case that as a purchaser I could add more to the bottom line by using my business methods.

As a purchaser, we would be hesitant in light of the current sector performance. It may well be, however, that we have a business that would benefit from this acquisition and would price it therefore as follows.

Assuming little fixed assets and stock to complicate the net asset position, we would pay pound for pound in cash the £250,000, assuming that the business could prove the recovery of the debts was assured. The profit streams seem rather more tenuous, however, and we would find a way to defer any more payment until we had proved that the transfer of the business was successful. The profits of £70,000, which equate to just over £50,000 after a nominal tax rate, would then attract a PEM of, say, around 5 as a starter for negotiation. The payment of this, however, would be deferred using a suitable earn-out instrument.

The total indicative offer that we would put forward would be £500,000, with half paid in cash, the other half paid in deferred cash or shares.

We hope that the above example shows how a deal is priced, and how the valuation is arrived at. It must be understood that this is not a precise science, and that one person's valuation may differ widely from another.

Tip: When the sellers of your target business suggest a valuation, ask how the figure is arrived at, and get it put in writing.

Here are eight more tips to discuss with your solicitor

1 Ensure that you pay as little as possible.
2 Remember that you will have control over your own business as well as the acquisition unless otherwise agreed (ie joint responsibilities).
3 Make sure the definition of net profit is very clearly defined. Ensure that the effects of currency fluctuations are carefully handled within the context of net profit calculations.
4 Try to anticipate regulatory or legislative changes that will depress the business' profits in the coming years.
5 Stipulate the amount of control that you will have over your 'new business' in the context of this arrangement.
6 Seek warranties and indemnities for any unforeseen or uncontrollable event wherever possible.
7 Make sure the cultures fit, as this is the most common form of failure to integrate.
8 Try to ensure key staff sign a lock-in document for the first 12 months.
9 Make sure any legal agreements do not restrict your ability to control or dispose of acquired company assets, for the good of the business.

picking your partners – cultivating your allies

Agreeing the deal

There are two major issues that we now urge you to identify. The first is the cultural fit, and the second concerns warranties and indemnities.

■ Cultural fit

The biggest single cause of failure to integrate within a purchaser's business, and therefore failure of earn-out, is the differing cultures within two businesses. If you have grown your business over a number of years, and have a core of loyal workers, it is likely that they, and you, will be comfortable about the way things are done.

Indeed, the unspoken values, the way that you react and address the needs of your employees may form the bond of trust that pre-empts any contract of employment.

Exposing the business, through purchase of another business may cause existing employees to feel less valuable. This can arrive in trivial form, such as dress code, informal habits of work and job titles, which may cause conflict between the two workforces.

This problem can be foreseen in every single sale or purchase of a business. It is vital that you spend enough time in the prospective seller's business prior to agreeing a sale, in order to identify any major cultural issues that will cause problems. *Listen to your instincts and don't paper over the cracks.*

Identify any concerns and make sure that you are satisfied that they have been addressed. If there is any inkling of a cultural mismatch, assume the worst, and either withdraw or seek warranties.

Understand that the business is unlikely to survive if the culture is not within a similar band to your own, as employees quickly leave and the essence of your business will be lost.

■ Due diligence on the acquired company

When you have agreed in principle the various terms of purchase there will then begin a process initiated by you called 'due diligence'. This usually requires your accountants to have uninterrupted access to the business to be acquired, and all of its historic records, for the purpose of finding anything unusual that might cause problems later.

The visit usually lasts a number of days, and will require the seller to spend a large percentage of their time in finding documents such as insurance policies, leases, employment contracts, tax returns, accounts information galore, sales figures and analysis, as well as supplier information, etc.

The findings will become the subject of a detailed report to you, to give you certain assurances that things are as they say they are. If the documentation is less than strong in certain areas, this may be raised as an issue in a subsequent meeting. Unless their business is hiding a great secret, or their interpretation of events does not support the reality, then the due diligence process is usually a lengthy formality. You can compare it to a professional check on a vehicle before you hand over the cheque.

■ Warranties and indemnities

In every purchase contract, there are clauses called warranties and indemnities, which the seller will be asked to agree to with a financial penalty wherever possible. The seller, on the other hand, will wish to avoid signing financial warranties.

The outcome is a position in the middle, but usually favouring the purchaser at the end of the day. The contract of sale is a document of shared risk.

Planning

Having been through the processes of due diligence, and spent time with the seller prior to commitment, it will be possible to agree a formalized plan of management—post acquisition.

When a company is acquired, it goes through a marked change and organizational crisis. The trauma experienced by all employees stems from the fact that the acquisition represents a clear break from the past, and they therefore need re-instructing as to their future role. It is well documented that most businesses may lose profits in the first 3–6 months after being acquired, and this is the major cause of the problem.

When you devise your plan, take into account the fact that most people will expect changes in the first few months. Indeed, if changes don't happen, you may find the same disruptive symptoms, as the perception will be that the purchaser is not interested in them! The human element to this plan is the most significant. All acquisitions start with the accounting systems, and then pause to find direction. Your plan must start with the people, and then keep going with the people, and not stop.

In our experience more goodwill is lost in the first two months by inaction than by anything else.

The plan that you propose must be all encompassing, and well documented to the best detail that you could deliver in the timescales. In the face of a good plan, the seller should welcome this dialogue, and it will also focus a little more clearly on any cultural difficulties.

General issues

Your professional advisers should highlight the obvious issues such as tax clearances and planning, and so we will simply list them here. Indeed, individual needs are so varied that this is the most that we can provide in this section.

Be careful about the employee service contracts terms, which may include some liabilities that you may not identify. If employees have served 20 years, the possibility of replacing them with the different skills that the merged business needs, or simply the rationalizing of common departments, will cost you a small fortune in redundancy payments or severance pay. Pay attention to the fringe benefits match between your business and the purchased business, as these can often cause discomfort between the two workforces.

Management strengths

The advantages and disadvantages of acquisitive growth will be particular to your own business. The single most important factor in the decision of whether to acquire or not is to question your strengths as a management team. Acquiring a business will be extremely time-consuming, and may require both you and other members of your team to be taken away from your core business for periods. If you get it right, the rewards can be forthcoming. Misjudge the situation, and the crisis that could result has been known to cripple the acquiring business financially.

Timing is everything in the acquisition stakes, for the cycle of your own business, and the stage of development of the acquired business.

BUILDING BLOCK 7

- Building partners in the market offers a number of advantages, such as increase in salesforce, joint marketing initiatives, joint customer bases and increased key customers.

- Select the right partners through product analysis, geography and adding value.

- Formulate a market vision with your new partner.

- Measure the partnership to see if it is a successful alliance.

- Connect IT and 'affinity link' with your partner's website.

- Ensure you have adequate virus protection/system security in place.

- Syndicate your alliances on the Internet to the virtual world.

- Identify appropriate market acquisitions to make long lasting alliances, which will add to your competitive edge.

- Consult a solicitor and understand the cost and steps that will be involved in your acquisition.

- Make sure there is a cultural fit as this is the biggest single cause of failure in acquisitions.

picking your partners – cultivating your allies

taking hard and fast action

8

Rapid change
management

Finance and accounting

Rapid change management

Estimating and forecasting

Organization design

*The ability to inspire passion and commitment and to motivate
your team to adapt to constant change is the key to success*

For many small businesses, change appears to be an accident! It creeps on the unwitting business leader, and manifests as a crisis. For us to build a small business that lasts we must accept continual change, and by accepting it, turn it into part of our everyday management approach.

Change in any environment is perceived to be risk and, as such, arouses fear as an emotive reaction. Your role as a business leader is to turn the job of managing change into an everyday process. By doing this, you will remove much of the emotion and replace it with fact, measurement and planning.

The process of change we have called RCM, which stands for Rapid Change Management. It is this process, which is based on years of research and application within many household named businesses, that we are now going to describe in detail.

RCM is for all team members to use and not simply the business leader.

RCM will teach the correct approach to strategic planning and developing good management skills. We have found that the following four skills will ensure success when implementing and managing change in your business.

1 Finance and accounting.
2 Rapid change management—getting results through teamwork planning.
3 Estimating and forecasting.
4 Organization theory.

FINANCE AND ACCOUNTING

Finance and accounting are the basic tools you need to understand when it comes to running any small business or enterprise. This section provides a brief overview of the topic and if you require further information or training please read *The Small Business Handbook* (Webb & Webb, Prentice Hall, 2001), which goes through training modules for the small business leader. Alternatively, contact your accountant who should be able to advise you on any matters relating to your business finances.

The following tries to demystify and explain simply the standard accounting terms that you will need to understand as a business leader. If you have difficulties in understanding finance and accounting, you will be unsuccessful in convincing financial institutions to lend you money, so it is imperative that you read and train yourself in this area until you feel confident that your knowledge is adequate.

- *The purpose of accounting* is to 'match expenses with current revenue', measured in the same time period (monthly or annually) to present a realistic picture of profits earned by the organization.
- *Management accounting*—the art of producing financial information in a format designed to help managers manage.
- *Budgeting*—the art of estimating the financial requirements (income and outgoing) for a 'future period' of an operation. Then, having made these estimates, to use them as a comparative measure against the actual expenditure. This is explained in more detail in the Action Plan (Form 3) explained later in this chapter.

Fixed or variable costs?

All operations have an element of expense related to time, and not linked to the work of the business. Rent, for example, is a charge for a period of time, not for the work being done. *Such period expenses are called 'fixed'.* That means the volume of work does not affect them directly.

There are other expenses that vary with the business activities. For example, materials are purchased for use in a product. As more goods are produced, more materials are consumed. *These costs are called 'variable'.*

How do we work out our breakeven position?

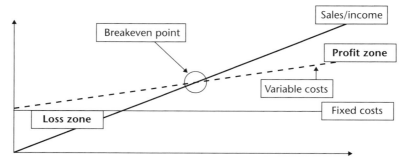

Fig. 8.1 ▪ **Fixed and variable costs against sales to plot the breakeven and profit zone**

Figure 8.1 shows the relationship between the fixed and variable costs against sales achieved. Overlaid on this cost graph is a line showing the relationship of sales versus fixed plus variable costs. The point where the lines cross is called *the breakeven point*. Above this point your business will make profit.

Management accounts

We have already referred to the term 'management accounts' as being financial information presented in a form which the manager can understand. Typically management accounts consist of:

▪ balance sheet;
▪ profit and loss account for the period;
▪ forward-looking cash flows;
▪ supporting detail.

■ Balance sheet, profit and loss account, and cash flow

Management accounts are produced periodically to show interested parties such as managers, lenders and shareholders the financial position of the company. It is usually prepared to the end of a given month, quarter or year and simply reflects the position at that time.

Compare it to taking a still photograph. What happens in the minutes to follow is that the position changes entirely and this can be the case with accounts as well. This snapshot in time is called the balance sheet and reflects the number of fixed assets, amounts owing to you (debtors), amounts in the bank (cash), amounts owed by you to others (creditors) and your borrowings (liabilities), all shown on a single piece of paper. *The balance sheet, to those who know how to read it, tells a story and provides clues as to the position of the company*.

For a given period, normally a month, quarter or year, the profit and loss account is also produced. This seeks to measure, sales or income and then lists the various deductions materials and overheads to arise at a net product or a net loss. This is a detailed statement of activity for the period and allows the manager to understand sales versus expenditure.

The forward-looking cash flow statements are not predicted bank balances. They simply indicate, based on a prediction of sales and expenditure, taking into account the payment profiles of your customers and suppliers, the average cash trend over the coming period.

To most business leaders, finance is something that is best left to accountants. In your small business built to last, however, finance will need to become one of your core skills.

For those of you who feel that you need a more in depth understanding of finance or benefit from using pre-written spreadsheets for profit and loss projections and cash flows, then we would point you again to the *Small Business Handbook*, by Webb and Webb which contains a CD-ROM with the spreadsheets that you will need.

In this example balance sheet (see Figure 8.2), we can see the addition of a PC to the asset register, bringing its total to £18,000. This suggests that this is a PC-based business and not manufacturing, with about six employees perhaps, as there will need to be a PC server as well.

We look separately at current assets which are different from fixed, as they can be turned into cash more easily. Debtors are the amounts owed to you by your customers, and the change in the period relates to new invoices less the debt collected, as these are no longer debtors, but cash.

BALANCE SHEET		
	Changes in this period	Year to date
Fixed Assets	£	£
PCs	2,000	18,000
Vehicles	nil	29,000
TOTAL	2,000	**47,000**
Current assets		
Debtors	20,000	60,000
Stock	nil	nil
Cash at hand	8,000	24,000
TOTAL		**84,000**
Current liabilities		
Creditors	26,000	84,000
Tax/PAYE	3,000	5,000
Short term loans		25,000
TOTAL		**114,000**
Net current assets		**(30,000)**
Long-term liabilities		5,000
Net asset position		**12,000**
Financed by:		
Share capital		100
Premium		2,000
Reserves		nil
Profit and loss	2,000	9,900
TOTAL		**12,000**

Fig. 8.2 ▪ Example of a balance sheet

The cash figure is a number which may not be your exact bank balance, as the balance sheet is a photograph and not a moving document.

Current liabilities show the amount you owe to your suppliers, known as creditors. Any tax or VAT owing, etc is also shown as current. Generally speaking, any amount owing in the next 12 months is shown as current liabilities. Longer than 12 months, and this is shown separately in *long-term liabilities*, but moves when it crosses the 12-month threshold.

Net current assets are found by deducting the current liabilities from the current assets. If a bracket is around the figure, then this is a negative amount. If current net asset is less than 1, then this company is likely to be under cash flow pressures. This is very often the case in small businesses.

The *net asset* position is fixed plus current assets, less current plus long-term liabilities, and should always be above 1. If this falls below 1, then you may be trading insolvently, and must seek immediate advice from your accountants.

The 'Financed by' section tells us how the company is financed. The share capital is often £100 for small businesses, but if more shares have been sold since company formation, then a share premium account may be showing. Reserves are retained profits from previous trading periods, and the profit and loss figures are drawn from the current cum to date for the period.

By adding up the total for the 'Financed by' section, you will notice that this is exactly the figure representing the net assets of the company. This demonstrates why it is called a balance sheet. These figures must always balance and be equal; otherwise there is an accounting error.

The example profit and loss accounts in Figure 8.3 relate to the current period as Month 4 in the 12 month year, this one being April. As we are in Month 4, we can do a quick check for the month by multiplying the current month figures by 4 in our heads. The result will tell us if we have made out of line expenditure in this month, or whether we have made savings compared to the previous averages.

The depreciation line is simply a percentage of the fixed assets, which is sometimes called the write down value. Things to look for in your business, is varying or reducing gross margins, caused by increasing materials costs or lower sales.

RAPID CHANGE MANAGEMENT

Rapid change management will also ensure the smooth transition of new technology within the business and its acceptance by the team.

PROFIT AND LOSS ACCOUNT		

Period of April 2001(Month 4)

	Current month	Year to date
	£	£
Sales	32,549	133,500
Materials	4,333	18,435
Gross margin	28,216	115,065
Overheads		
Salaries	11,800	46,500
PAYE	5,500	19,300
Motor expenses	3,100	14,300
Rent/rates	1,200	4,800
Telephone	450	1,850
Subscriptions	50	200
Equipment hire	1,450	5,880
Utilities	320	1,220
Other	1,546	7,815
Depreciation	800	3,300
Total	**26,216**	**105,165**
Net profit/loss	**2,000**	**9,900**

Fig. 8.3 ■ **Example of a profit and loss account**

Given these forward looking skills, RCM then brings them together in a defined process to allow the business leader to implement process-based change to a timescale. This team approach can be used for planning and budgeting or for any type of project work—including all forms of consultation and participation required for development work. RCM is used to accelerate the development of the organization, whether it is a profit or not-for-profit operation. This programme makes it possible to use, and also to teach this method to others, on-the-job, to achieve agreed objectives.

Getting results

Results depend on the manager's commitment to get the right things done. His commitment can be reinforced and encouraged by 'agreement' at the top and the willingness of those around him to 'accept' and respond to the need for change. We have developed a straightforward process which delivers a practical 'team approach' to getting things started and enabling ongoing control. Results can be delivered within a specified timescale.

RCM is a system designed to speed up the process of initiating and controlling change within an organization. It is a straightforward procedure to improve the use of time in setting targets, objectives and controlling results to schedules and budgets.

RCM is a unique approach for diagnosing problems and prescribing remedies, which carry the conviction and commitments of those who will be involved in actually obtaining results.

This is made possible by systematically breaking down inter-personal barriers, eliminating perceptions of unfairness and threat, gathering relevant information and making it possible to use the full brain power of those working together as a 'team'.

A detailed guide to use

■ What is RCM?

RCM is short for rapid change management, and as the title infers, is a method for managing situations and intended situations, by a team input vehicle.

You have all heard the saying, 'two heads are better than one', and to take this a stage further, a team of professionals have more resource and intellect/ideas than an individual.

An RCM session must always have a statement of intention, ie a goal or required end result. It is run as a meeting, excluding all interruptions from operational work activity.

■ When do we use it?

RCM is used in any situation where:

- the problem solver requires assistance;
- the problem is too complex for one person;

- change is forecast as the end result;
- the outcome will affect your team members.

How many times have you been involved in a change situation without consultation, and believed the final outcome is not the best one? The use of RCM ensures that the input, and therefore agreement of *all* of the key team members is included and acted upon. Change, therefore, is much smoother and uninterrupted because it is given the support of all.

■ What is the format for use?

The format for use revolves around a pre-chosen subject. For example 'we have a new product that we would like to launch in the most effective way possible'.

Data and ideas are collected over a period of time, and then analyzed in the RCM session. The data is gathered as *'planning issues'*, and represents all employees' views about the given subject.

The data is then categorized into sections:

- product;
- process;
- customer;
- distribution;
- finance;
- administration.

It is very important to understand that the information gathered in the planning issues is of a potentially sensitive nature, and any analysis is done with *no threat to any individual. If an individual's name appears, strike it out and replace it with the person's job function.*

From the categories described above, the planning issues form a theme from which a sub-section of the team then assign a title to the group of issues. Use Figure 8.5 Recommended Action (Form 2). This title is representative of the issues, but should not seek to address them individually nor solve them. The team members should try to look for the bigger picture as an *action title*.

For example, the regular refusal by individuals to take calls on the telephone, and the inadequacies of a message system, should translate into an *action title* such as '*improve communications systems.*'

Look at the reasons and the method of fix, not at the symptoms (Figure 8.4 Planning Issue Form 1).

The team then reconvenes the RCM committee, and the *action titles* are read out. The titles individually are agreed at group level, as being worthy titles and worth pursuing with management time. The exact wording for a title may be refined at this stage, and agreed by the group.

For example 'improve communication systems' might be amended to 'change communication systems'.

When the action titles have been agreed, each RCM committee member is asked to contribute a one-line comment which is added on the note section on Form 2. These comments are usually helpful suggestions, or possible problems associated with this action title. Each member is allowed one comment per action title only.

The *strategic action titles*, as they are now known, are published in a list and distributed to the RCM team. The chairperson then calls for volunteers to take the action programmes and to work on them to solution. The final assignation of these titles then takes place and the chairperson will ensure that all titles have an 'owner'. This list is published and agreed.

From this point on, we move to the action plan (see Figure 8.6) (Form 3). With the intended action plan, after careful consideration, we can now produce a cost model of the likely spend or saving that this project will produce.

Preparation before the RCM meeting

'*Think*' is the only preparation you will need.

- Think about the company, the people, the departments, and the attitudes.
- Think about your weaknesses, but don't forget your strengths; you have a lot of those.
- Think about your customers, without which you wouldn't be here.

- Think about the future, and the exciting plans you have.
- Think about smiles, and what motivates people.
- Think about costs, and what is and is not possible.
- Think long term, but don't forget the present.

Issue the statement of work to all of the people from whom you wish to have an input. This can involve all of your team or just a part or even extend to your suppliers, partners or customers. Request their completion of as many Planning Issues (Figure 8.4) as they can submit. Remember everybody's input no matter how simple must form part of this process if you are to achieve the culture of recognition and fair play.

> **Tip:** *The easiest way to collect multiple Planning Issues is to set up a sealed collection box which is only opened on the day of the RCM meeting. It is vital that you make it clear that all Planning Issues must be submitted anonymously.*

Suggested RCM agenda

1 Chairperson's opening speech, declaring the intention of the session.
2 Open the *Planning Issues Box*, spreading out the contents
3 Pass each and every issue around the table in an orderly manner. Read carefully, understand, and sign. When you read an issue, and come across a name, delete it and make it impersonal. This makes the process a non-threatening one to any individual.
4 Once the issues have been signed by all, the issues are then numbered sequentially, to ensure that *all* of the planning issues are addressed and taken into account. By this process, no single view of any individual is left out. Remember that every opinion is valid and equal.
5 The issues are then read aloud, and sorted one by one as a group into the following categories:
  - *Product.* Is it product related?
  - *Process.* Is it related to a process that is definable?
  - *Customer.* Is it to do with a customer or related customer function?

- *Distribution.* Is it to do with the distribution processes?
- *Finance.* The accounts department or company structure?
- *Administration.* Is it a people issue?

6 Once the issues are divided into the above categories, then teams are formed against the categories, eg:

Product team	....
Process team	....
Customer team	....
Distribution team	....
Finance team	....
Administration team	....

Take the group of issues as defined by the categories above, as allocated to your name.

Find your working partner(s), and decide from which office you are going to work.

This may be an opportunity for coffee, but it is *not* an opportunity to take messages or to make phone calls. Splitting into different offices is for your convenience only.

With your partner(s), read the issues from one group at a time. Decide what lies at the root cause of the issue. Is it real, or a symptom of a deeper problem? Group together any like or similar topic issues, and attempt to define the overall strategy that will address these issues.

Do not attempt to solve the problems. The purpose of the exercise is to form titles that will be used by a different study group, in order to put a solution in place. For example, 'Lost delivery notes, misplaced stock, untested equipment, British standards non-conformities', all listed on separate Planning Issues, does not equate to '*hire an extra warehouse man, or fire the existing one*'. Instead, a likely title would be something like 'improve warehouse procedures or start quality checking procedures'.

The title should read as a verb, ie

- start;
- improve;
- stop;
- develop;
- create;

- formalize;
- complete.

Then the subject, ie, what it is all about. Finished with the format, eg:

- programme;
- procedure;
- description;
- operation;
- manual;
- document.

When the issues have been categorized and grouped, (it is permissible to have one issue trigger a whole category) then look at the summarized results.

Is there any other Action Programme that is perhaps not covered by a Planning Issue, that your team may wish to see as an Action Programme anyway?

Using the Recommended Action (Figure 7.5), write down the Action Titles, one per page, until you have finished.

7 Re-form as a large group as soon as you have finished. The group will now present the Action Titles, one group at a time, and explain how the title derived. The RCM group as a whole have an opportunity to ask or recommend a change to the wording as appropriate, or to accept the Action Title in its entirety. *At the end of this session, the RCM team will have taken ALL the employees' views, analyzed them, formed and agreed Actions, and documented them.*

8 The chairperson will now ask for each member of the team to put your name against the Action Titles that interest them. Assignation of titles will require team members to spend additional time in this area, in order to become the study group that eventually solves this problem.

The chairperson will now, at his or her discretion, assign *all* of the Action Titles for completion to the individual or teams.

9 As a group, each assigned Action Title will be allocated to an Owner. One by one, each member of the group reads aloud the Action Titles. At this point, the owner of the title asks each and every person for comments, ideas or criteria which he or she will record. The owner is *not* allowed to agree or disagree and the team as a

whole is *not* allowed to debate. This process will take the unencumbered and independent view of each individual.

This RCM process is now complete.

How to use the action plan (Form 3)

So, you now have the assigned *action titles*. You have a fairly good idea of how to go about addressing this. *But*:

- How much will it cost?
- When do we spend this money?
- Who will approve this ?
- How does it affect the company overall?
- Will it produce a saving?

All these questions and more are brought to light when the completion of the financial summary known as the Action Plan (Figure 8.6) is performed. See the model form on page 144 for an example of how to complete.

PLANNING ISSUE (FORM 1)

SHORT TITLE _____

	Present	or	Future	
Strength	☐		Opportunity	☐
Weakness	☐		Threat	☐

● Description or statement of issue

● References, sources or example

● Ranges of possible action

Fig. 8.4 ■ RCM Planning Issue form

RECOMMENDED ACTION (FORM 2)   ACTION PLAN NO. _____

ACTION PLAN TITLE _____

Verb	Subject	Modifier

Notes

Purpose and procedures of this form

Determine total requirements objectively and produce a comprehensive listing of actions covering all aspects of the operation. Complete one form for one action. Action Titles should be:

- clear in scope and intent;
- manageable—assignable to one person and budgetable;
- ensuring—not temporary;
- significant—deserve the personal attention of the team member;
- simple—grammatical construction as shown below.

To help you, here are some examples, in each category, in no particular order.

Verb*	Subject	Modifier
Create	Purchasing procedures	Activity
Start	Management training	Programme
Stop-Divest	Business planning	System
Develop	New product	Operation
Improve	Sales expansion	Project
Establish	IT review	Task
Introduce	Communications	Function
Accelerate	Acquisition	Department
Expand	Customer care	Organisation

*Do not use: Plan, Review, Study, Analyze

Fig. 8.5 ■ RCM Recommended Action form

ACTION PLAN (FORM 3)   DEVELOPMENT

WORK STATEMENT   ACTION PLAN NO _____
                                                                SECTION _____

1. Study-Phase _____

                                                        Short title _____

2. Planning-Phase _____

                                                        Assignee: Control _____
3. Implementation-Phase _____   Action _____

PROGRAMME (Cost & Schedule)

Phase	Jan	Feb	Mar	Apr	May	Jun	Jul	Aug	Sep	Oct	Nov	Dec	20_ J F M A M J J A S O N D	20_ J F M A M J J A S O N D	20_ J F M A M J J A S O N D	20_ J F M A M J J A S O N D
1																
2																
3																
Budget	£												£	£	£	£

RESULTS (Sales & Savings)

	20_												20_	20_	20_	20_
1																
2																
3																
Budget	£												£	£	£	£

ASSUMPTIONS

CONTROL SYSTEM

1
2
3

Fig. 8.6 ■ **RCM Action Plan**

■ Action Plan (Form 3) A guide to use

What is form 3?

Form 3, which looks time-consuming and complex to complete, is in fact a very simple *financial diary*.

When used correctly, it will ask the creator to consider the costs associated with any particular project, and to accurately map them into the fiscal year. From this chart, we can see the points of expenditure, or indeed the points of saving, and then map these into the five-year fiscal statement in the relevant spreadsheet. At any one time then, the financial planning teams can see the picture of spend for that year. The company as a whole can see how to react to these periods of spend or save, and adjust accordingly. We therefore have a very proactive organization, with no nasty surprises!

The Form 3 method of financial planning can only be as accurate as the person completing it. The company may make decisions based on the data that *you* prepare. It is not a game, or an annoyance. This is serious, and meaningful, and should be done with care, or not at all.

How can I get excited about a form that looks so awful?

- **Stop** looking at the form.
- **Start** thinking about the company, the expansion, the people, and the projects.
- **Think** about the extra staff, the new PCs, software and building.
- **Think** about the new opportunities, new markets, new subsidiary companies.
- **Think** about the rewards, the Christmas party, the promotion prospects.

Why are we doing this?

We are learning to plan. Because if we don't plan, we can be likened to a blind man—we don't know where we are going, why, when, how much will it cost us, or whether we can we afford it? We will not survive as a fast-growing, profitable company; we will slump into mediocrity at best, go bust at worst.

So, how do I plan?

You plan by estimating.

- using historical information;
- using trend analysis;
- using ratios:
  - between costs and people
  - between costs and sales
  - between costs and a mixture of both of these
  - fixed costs, no matter how many people or sales
- using gut reaction.

How should I start to plan?

By following the simple guidelines above.

- You must gather all information around you.
- Look at *all* of the possible costs associated with this event.

Example: *Let us plan for an additional person in your department.* Answer the following questions.

- What does he or she do?
- Is the job a revenue-earning one?
- What commission or overtime is paid?
- Is a car needed?
- Cost out:
  - private healthcare (around £720 per year)
  - pension (five per cent of net basic)
  - employer's National Insurance (ten per cent of basic).

- Cost out a desk and chair if needed.
- Cost a PC if needed.
- Mobile telephone?
- Put a cost in for use of the telephone.
- What about stationery, pens, paper, books?
- Are you ever going to train them externally?

How much?

If you carry out the above calculation, you may well ask: 'Is that really how much we spend on *one* person?' The answer is *yes*! It's just that we hardly ever break down the individual costs per person. We say blandly that our stationery spend is £6,000 per year. Our cars cost us £18,000 per year. We accept these as *overheads*, but whose overheads? All of our overheads is the answer.

This is how we make up the company's budgetary spend per year. We don't wave a finger in the air, and say 'umm, about £6,000', or 'err, £18,000 will do'.

It is an exacting science of estimation. I would ask you to consider all pertinent costs, because we can always issue lower budgets to save money, it is much more difficult to find extra money later, and try and pretend it is all part of the plan.

So, what is the format for this planning?

The format is by nominals. 'Oh no!' I hear you cry, 'not that horrible accounts stuff again, now I know I'm not going to be any good at this'. Dispel this myth now.

The accounts department is simply the allocation of little bits of money we have spent in certain areas, to a box, where we can total it and understand where our money has gone *historically*.

We do this by allocating a *nominal code*, or four digit number to a particular department. The number and the description of the department is chosen at the beginning of the year by the accounts department.

Thus we have a pre-printed *chart of accounts*. This chart should be the Planner's Guide to Success, and is to be thought of as the ultimate crib sheet! For each bit of planned expenditure, you will find a nominal code to put this against.

Why is it done this way?

Because at the end of everybody's planning session, we then have a standard protocol to amalgamate all of the costs. In other words, we have a standard costing model which when added, gives a sensible and universally readable picture.

Do I plan alone then?

Before you are able to plan alone, there is a piece of group work to be done.

- The overall sales level has to be disclosed.
- The number of people has to be agreed as a group.
- The criteria, or requirements for the year have to be understood.
- The ramp up, or the monthly sales forecast is disclosed.

This last item will ensure that you can accurately forecast your people requirements.

That's OK—now what?

You have finished planning! You have the people mapped out, the dates of taking them on, and the subsequent costs associated. You understand where they will sit, what sort of work they will do, and their work related costs in terms of PC, desk, chair, training, cars, etc.

What format is it in? The chances are that it is either on scrap paper, a hocked spreadsheet, or some other equally unfriendly medium.

To simplify the planning process, we take the information you have devised, and pop it on to a Form 3 (Figure 8.6). Let us now take a look at the Form 3.

Look at Figure 8.6. From the top left then:

The *work statement* shows three areas of text space.

1 *Study phase*. Are there any costs, either capital or expense, which are associated with the studying of a project? An example of this is where a piece of software is bought for trial, maybe not to be used if it doesn't do the job.
2 *Planning phase*. Any costs to do with the planning of a project. An example may be where you visit a supplier or number of suppliers to plan the project.
3 *Implementation phase*. This is actually carying out the project.

The above three areas should have text in them, describing your activities in the relevant spaces.

To the top right of Form 3 (Figure 8.6), there is space for the Action Plan number. This is needed when you are in fact planning from a TAM issue. You will then complete the short title and the assignee sections below it.

The middle of the document is reserved for the chart of plan. This is the area where the planner has the ability to record the intended costs. The format is using the delta symbol, linked by a straight line to indicate the endurance of the activity, ended by another delta symbol.

If the activity lasts over a period of time, then the delta ends must start and finish where the planner thinks is fit.

This marking procedure must be used for all three areas of activity, ie, study, planning and implementation.

When the delta lines have been plotted on the Form 3, the planner must then allocate the costs associated with the activity alongside the delta bar. The format for these costs is by *nominal* code as described above. If there is insufficient room for all of the codes, then use two forms and split the costs onto a duplicate Form 3.

The programme then might look like this:

Month

	Jan	Feb	Mar	Apr	May
Study	V———————V		7220 Motor expenses 28		
			5515 Staff Expenses 15		
Planning		V———————V	7450 Training 400		
			5515 Staff Expenses 120		
Implementation			V———————————————V		
			7230 Lease of equipment		
			2000/yr.		
			7450 Training 450		

The scenario is that you find a requirement for an automated process within the company.

Phase 1: Study. You travel to several suppliers to ascertain the suitability of the software.

Phase 2: Planning. You book yourself onto a training course to finally select the solution, and use one night in a hotel.

Phase 3: Implementation. You have selected the software; you now buy the hardware complete with software on a lease, and then train the rest of the department in-house, using an external trainer.

Look at the scenario, and relate this to the *nominals* used, and the costs. You may feel there may be additional costs, but the above is for illustration only.

That looks so easy though!

It is! There is no mystery to planning, just forethought and method. A simple translation to the Form 3, and there you have it!

What is the difference between capital and expenses?

The difference is this: A *capital* item, is a piece of hardware, be it a desk, chair, computer, building, or car. When these items are purchased they are to become *fixed assets*. Fixed assets are things that you can sell later if you wish.

An *expense*, is a one off, non-recoverable thing, such as expenses, legal costs, staff salaries, training costs, pensions, entertainment, etc. You cannot sell them again, because they are gone, eaten, or used up!

When you make something a fixed asset, it is usually over £200 in value. It then becomes eligible to be depreciated. Usually, for example:

- vehicles are depreciated at 25 per cent per year
- office equipment is depreciated at 15 per cent per year.

Each item that you buy which is a fixed asset will have a depreciation charge at the appropriate rate, allocated to it. It is very easy to set up a written depreciation table as shown in Table 8.1.

Table 8.1 Example of a written depreciation table

	Year 1	Year 2	Year 3	Year 4	Year 5
Car (8000 new)	2000(6000)	1500(4500)	1125(3375)	843.75(2531.25)	632.81
PC (2000 new)	300(1700)	255(1445)	216.75(1228.25)	184.24(1044)	156.60

The figures under the years are the amounts you charge to the depreciation nominal. The reducing balance, or the *book value* can be seen in the brackets. Remember the percentages for the two types of asset, 25 per cent and 15 per cent.

The *'Results' section* is simply a translation of the net costs, capital and expenses into a summary form. The control system may be a procedure, or it may be the Board of Directors. The assumptions may be that a certain level of sales is achieved.

So completing Form 3 should not be as difficult as you first thought!

Figure 8.7 summarizes the RCM section phase.

FORM 1
Ideas, problems, opportunities and future threats. Emotion or logic.

Form 1s are used to gather opinions and information, as well as ideas and problem statements, anonymously from the data group. This group can be employees, suppliers, customers or stakeholders to the business or to the process. All FORM 1s are counted, none are discarded.

RCM PROCESS
Is driven using principles of fair play to a determined structure, replacing emotion with logical approaches and process.

The RCM committee accepts all Form 1s regardless of content, thereby accepting every individual's point of view. The RCM process guides the committee to make common themes, categorize and then devize action plans or projects to address the larger issue.

ACTION PLANS
Suggestions for projects or activity.

Action plans are devized and assessed as worthy of management time. These are then worked up into projects with costs and defined terms of reference. A project leader is assigned and financial impact statements rolled into the planning process. Timescales are agreed.

FORM 3
Rolling financial statements which measure the effect of the action plans.

Budgets are reviewed and approved in order to complete the development project. All activity is published to the Form 1 providers such that inclusion is promoted and a sense of fair play and an acceptance culture are generated. This in itself often leads to a performance uplift in the business.

This activity is reviewed and published until complete.

Fig. 8.7 ▓ RCM – overview of the process

ESTIMATING AND FORECASTING

This is the developed skill to make:

- cost and/or price estimates;
- man-hour estimates;
- budget and income forecasts;
- planned projects.

Managing change requires coping with uncertainty. The reduction of uncertainty is achieved by developing skill in estimating and forecasting. The professional learns how to use the Gompertz S Curve for forecasting, along with standard learning curves in setting costs and income estimates, man-hour estimates to any statement of work. They learn how to make cost/benefit forecasts and to layout simple plans and budgets based on action programmes summaries.

This training programme in Chapter 9 should be treated as an ordinary capital investment, as it is designed to give a return on the investment (ROI) greater than any other capital investment opportunity open to an organization. For more information see Chapter 9 *Driving sales*.

ORGANIZATION DESIGN

This is the skill required to design the people structure and forecast future structural changes required.

A team member, to be effective should understand organization theory and design, so as to make those recommendations that improve communications, report lines and team work. The manager learns how to design an organization structure, evolve the right structure for his own organization, and to forecast future structural changes that will be required. He is given a background in organization theory and some history of management systems. For more information see Chapter 10 *Market Masters*.

BUILDING BLOCK 8

How to manage change in your business

1 Prepare:
- the RCM committee defines the problem area;
- a team leader and executive team are appointed to carry out the RCM procedure;
- all employees with a contribution to make send in their views to the team.

Planning Issue Form 1 required.

2 RCM workshop:
- the team sorts the views and makes preliminary recommendations;
- the team refines and reviews the recommendations;
- the leader obtains a team commitment to the recommendations.

Recommended Action Form 2 required.

3 Presentation.
- Agreed actions are proposed to the Managing Director for approval.

Action Plan Form 3 required.

4 Get results:
- the MD approves actions after alteration, if necessary;

5 Control:
- after an agreed interval, the team assembles to control and assess progress and initiate corrective actions if required.

6 Understanding the finance and accounting in your business will ensure you can plan and forecast your business accurately.

7 Study your management accounts regularly.

8 Train and develop your knowledge on all matters of finance in the business.

rapid change management

9

Driving sales

Sales forecasting

Bringing it together

Qualify your prospects

Attributes of good salespeople

Active listening

Cadence questioning

I n our small business built to last, we have already looked in detail in Chapter 6 *Focus on the real customer* as to the various ways of identifying and reaching out to the real customer.

The real customer, you will recall, is one with whom we can have a long-standing relationship, and become partners within their business and from whom we can derive a quality earning stream.

We assessed the desirability of becoming very close to these customers and retaining them in the long term, by using various technologies and financial tools. In this chapter, we turn our attention to the people within our business who will interface, propose and win deals with these customers.

As the business leader in a small business it is highly likely that you will also fall into this category, as one of the key roles of a small business leader is to sell and manage sales.

A selling operation in any business will assume the shape of an 'S' curve over time. Often referred to as the 'Gompertz curve', it demonstrates how the volume of sales starts small, can grow rapidly and then reach a plateau, which indicates that newness is required (see Figure 9.1).

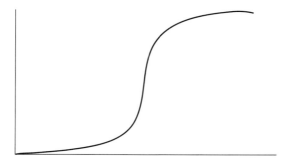

Fig. 9.1 ■ Example of a Gompertz curve

This 'newness' may take the form of:

- strategic direction;
- new products;
- new people;
- new partners.

What the S curve theorists often fail to tell you is what happens if you don't achieve this newness at the point you reach the top of the S or the plateau. The answer is that your S curve turns into a bell curve (see Figure 9.2). This means a same shape decline unless you adopt actions to take on newness.

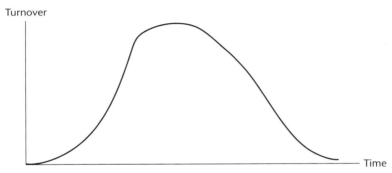

Fig. 9.2 ▨ Example of a bell curve

The name we are going to put to this bell curve is your base business.

At the height of your sales success, if you do nothing different, look for no new customers, stay the same as you did in the previous period, than your business will fall away.

The time it takes for your base business to decline can be alarmingly short and is often underestimated. To see for yourself, try looking at your customer list from just 12 months ago. When you have those names, look for them again in the last 6 months' sales data. Where they appear, record the revenue. Now plot your own bell curve. All of the new customers, that you have serviced in the last 6 months, which did not appear in your year old list, can be brought together under the title of 'development business'.

Ongoing development business is essential when we build a small business to last (see Figure 9.3).

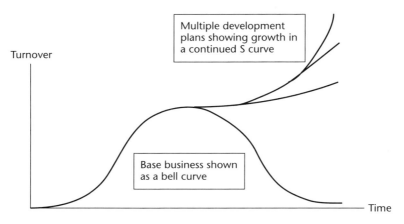

Fig. 9.3

Each piece of development business will be smaller than your total base business but will, over a period of time, become the base business! However, at the time it is first developed it can be measured, almost as a single project. You can derive the same measurements and comparisons of its profitability and resource requirements as you can with your total business.

Example: Planning future development business should also be done separately to your base business planning. For example, if you hire a new sales person, you can apply a financial plan to his or her performance. For example, if they earned £36,000 per annum, and did not make any sales until month 3, moving past breakeven in month 5, then you could expect to incur a salary loss of at least, say, £12,000 before your business starts to reap the benefits.

In addition to salary costs, there will be of course, expenses, car, National Insurance, benefits, etc that compound this problem.

Similarly, a new marketing seminar, which costs £5,000 in month one, returning 50 sales enquiries on which you close 5 in the two months that follow at a sales price of £10,000 will reap a £15,000 profit over the quarter. We can take the profit and loss analysis to the next vital stage and measure the impact upon cash flow.

In our business, we should have a constant eye on the base business and a number of planned, well-thought-out and executed development projects that maintain our S curve and reduce the risks of becoming a bell curve.

SALES FORECASTING

The above section, describing base business plus multiple development business leads us nicely to the application of this principle in sales forecasting. In our small business, one of the largest risks to our future success is our ability to plan and forecast our sales.

Sales forecasting is incredibly difficult to get right in small businesses, for three reasons:

- we often have very little history in terms of years in business on which to base our assumptions;
- because small business has a high proportion of development sales each year than our sales results can often be lumpy;
- having experienced some success, entrepreneurs develop a natural tendency to be optimistic, which results in overstated sales in planning.

We would like you to consider your sales planning in two sections: first, to plan your base business; second, to add your development business, project by project.

Base business planning

Below are some ideas that you may wish to adopt in the process of planning your base business, or your sales revenue line during the annual budgeting.

- Use any historical data that you may have at your disposal and extrapolate.
- Look at individual customers, and even ask them what level of spend that they anticipate with you next year.

This can be a valuable insight as to the state of the relationship that you have with your customer. If the level of sales has decreased from the previous year, for example, you have an early opportunity to visit them to ask why. If the customer becomes cagey with you, sound the alarm bells and make a quick appointment with your contact. They may surprise you and, based upon your excellent service, tell you of a planned increase in business with your company next year.

- If you can approach as many as 80 per cent of your major clients, the forecast for your base business can start to assume some accuracy.
- Assume some loss of business, or the non-repeat of certain key contracts that you fulfilled last year. Don't delude yourself that you are able to retain all of this business.
- Balance your forecast against the prevalent market conditions. If the world market is in gross price decline, be aware that you will have to make more sales to achieve the same level of turnover as last year.

You will end up with a base plan that reflects the level of sales that you would make if you just do next year what you did this year. (Please don't allow for any growth and plan for this figure to decline over the 12-month period.)

Development business

This is your opportunity to plan from a blank piece of paper. Please refer to Chapter 8 *Rapid change management* and consider using Recommended Action (Form 2) as the basis for recording your development projects.

You may have several pieces of development business for example, increased marketing spend may be one, the hire of additional sales people may be another, a new product may be yet another. Each development plan must be performed separately and independently. If you do not do this, you are highly likely to distort your sales projections, as you optimistically take the new product, the additional marketing and the salesperson and apply a higher expectation to the three jointly as you would have done by adding up the three plans separately.

Development business can be any activity that changes what you have or are about to do from now on. If you believe that the hiring of a salesperson will help grow your business, then this plan is development. Please don't forget that salespeople take time to settle in and may not win deals in their first few months. When they start to produce sales, apply their target gradually over the next 12 months, as to apply a full target any sooner may lead to overstatement. This development plan will have an estimated sales line against which you will need to apply costs.

The true costs of hiring a salesperson are normally understated.

The costs relating to the salesperson as individuals are compounded by an increase in overheads when you hire additional people. For example the salesperson's costs in the opening months may be a recruitment fee, business cards and stationery, car, pension, health scheme, computer, a sales database against which he or she will market, a mobile telephone, travel expenses and the use of the existing team's time to induct into the company, its products and methods. (Refer to Chapter 8 *Rapid change management*, and use the Action Plan (Form 3) to plan all of your development projects.)

You will then have a series of development plans which will effectively make or cost you money. Add them up only at the end, and even then sanitize the numbers so as not to be over optimistic.

By using this base plus development planning method, we found that we subjected ourselves to a greater scrutiny than we would otherwise have done, and we recommend it to you.

The main difficulty in planning accurately within a small business is that you won't have been in business for very long, and the historical data from which you might make certain assumptions is less than reliable.

The development business can only draw on tiny comparators from previous years and if this is not the extension of an existing activity, then best 'guesstimates' may be your only recourse. You must ensure that you explore every option to base your projections on something proven or concrete. If this is not possible, then err very carefully on the side of caution.

BRINGING IT TOGETHER

We hope you have taken notes in earlier chapters and that you are using a spreadsheet or a PC-based planning package in order to record your business financial plan. We suggest for ease of administration that the sales plan is itemized as the base sales plus the series of development sales expected as per the above plans. In this way you will be able to plot your actual against your budget in future months and with a little extra work you can attribute a sales actual to each development plan budget.

Adopting this method will provide you with an insightful view of your business as the months go by, in addition to providing you with detailed information to support your future planning activity.

Using this method, it will be possible to quickly identify any failing development projects and take prompt action to reduce or eliminate any of the planned costs against this project.

At a supporting statement, you should always attempt to introduce resource or overhead behind the sales event (the obvious exception is the salesperson). Small businesses commonly suffer from lower profitability because overhead structures are introduced early to support sales that never arrive.

Once you have performed all of the above on a scientific basis, apply your 'gut feel' factor to the plans. Can you really make the numbers? Don't fool yourself, you are kidding nobody except yourself. If you are using the format of the spreadsheet, beware using the extrapolation function, whereby you click on the cell, and drag the value (or, even worse, the formula for increase) across the entire 12 months. Each year has a holiday season, end of year sales, etc, and so you must adjust your sales line for these conditions. It is easy to say that August won't be as bad this year as last, but unless you sell deckchairs or air-conditioning units, the August holiday season, and others besides, will have a negative effect, and you must plan for lower sales during this time.

Now we would like to move on to talk about the monthly forecast of sales that we would encourage you to perform each and every month as a discipline. By performing this assessment, you achieve the following:

- understand how your business is faring by comparing to the annual sales budgets;
- accurately plan for extra or fewer staff depending upon real numbers;
- send a message to your staff as to the importance of selling, and the dependence upon the customer;
- show the sales team that there is no hiding place from your understanding and scrutiny.

In our small business built to last, we now have the best chance of successful planning using our base plus development planning methods. You would have noticed that we have referred to using the process-driven forms in the rapid change management approach. By using these forms we would hope you will see additional benefits of adopting RCM as a culture within your business and not as a one-off exercise.

We will now follow the measurement trial from best practice planning into practical and essential sales measurement. Earlier in this book we have established the theme of planning, based upon information and facts which give us the highest probability of building a business that lasts.

Coming out of the eye of the storm you will be confronted by a fast-moving, technology based, constantly changing world. Our success in selling will be enhanced by these technologies, although in some markets, technology will still be a way of securing a qualified face-to-face appointment. The old values and theories of selling will not disappear simply because of Internet and e-mail, and because time is so precious it will increase our need to present effectively, once we have a sales appointment.

Ask yourself this question: when was the last time, you the business leader, and your sales team attended a formal sales training course, or refresher seminar? If you have ever been on a sales training course, it is likely to be some time ago.

driving sales

As part of our planning to be a business that lasts, regular refresher sales courses are essential to maintain a high performance sales operation.

As a test for your business, select three prospects that you believe you have a reasonable chance of winning and apply the following qualifying test.

QUALIFY YOUR PROSPECTS

Here are the ten questions to ask yourself or your salesperson, before accepting it as a qualified deal for next month's sales. You must score 80 points or more.

1	Do you know for sure that you are talking to the decision-maker?	(10 Points)
2	Does your customer have budget for spend already approved?	(10 Points)
3	Do you know who your competition is?	(10 Points)
4	Has your customer received a written quote from you?	(10 Points)
5	Do you have free access to the directors of your customer?	(10 Points)
6	Do you have a diarized 'close' meeting set up yet	(10 Points)
7	have you done business with this customer before?	(10 Points)
8	Has the customer given you feedback from your proposal?	(10 Points)
9	Do you know on what criteria your customer will select suppliers?	(10 Points)
10	Have you handled all of the customer's objections yet?	(10 Points)

This is a tough list, but unless your sales approach has tackled all of the above issues, you are operating a hit-and-miss salesforce, and the results will be gained on luck and not on forecasting and professionalism.

You may like to issue this checklist as permanent qualification criteria for all your new prospects. In this way your sales efforts will be operated from the most solid platform and will also make best use of its time in terms of qualifying prospects to either do business with real customers, or to walk away from commodity buyers.

As your small business achieves growth over time, you may have a number of sales people working for the company. The attributes of each salesperson are different, as sales is an art form based on personality and not on science. It is the application of the theory, with enthusiasm, which makes for a good salesperson. As you engage with a number of different types of customer, have you yet discovered which salespeople have the right attributes for the right customer?

In performing this analysis, you are also to dig deep into the persona of the salesperson simply by taking adequate detailed measurements. As in earlier chapters, your use of technology is essential in order to:

■ achieve your first set of measurements which may be the most difficult;

■ continuously update this information with minimal effort.

Let us now look at some of the measurements which are easily derived from an effective information system.

Log each sale individually, and classify the following information:

■ turnover;

■ gross margin;

■ type of customer by market sector, ie retail, banking, manufacturing, etc;

■ order frequency of the customer;

■ type of product and whether this is a planned or distress purchase;

■ size of customer, by turnover and number of employees.

By salesperson, analyze the following:

■ total turnover in the month;

■ total gross margin in the month;

■ number of deals in the month;

■ type of product sold to which sector customers;

■ whether the targets have been met for the month (see below for target setting);

- the anticipated orders for the coming month and then for the following quarter;
- the sales by location and the time of the month in which they were received ie, week numbers 1–4;
- expenses per salesperson per month;
- the rate of sales closed versus the number of meetings attended—this should be expressed as a percentage and called the 'close rate' of the salesperson.

ATTRIBUTES OF GOOD SALESPEOPLE

During your work in the earlier chapters you may have identified with the right sizing and the expansion sectors of Chapter 3, when securing your business for the future, you need to consider a skills audit of your existing team to ensure that they have the necessary skills and characteristics to adopt new products, services and to embrace changes, in your business and in your customers' businesses.

In this section we will only be considering salespeople in your business. For more information regarding your business' entire workforce, and how to optimize the company's performance, please see Chapter 10 *Market Masters*.

This is the same audit that you will perform when conducting an interview of a possible sales recruit. It is absolutely essential that a small business, if it is to be built to last, must make as few mistakes as possible in the hiring of all of its staff, but especially its salespeople. Salespeople are probably the highest-paid resource in your business and you must ensure an adequate return from each of them.

Some of the basic characteristics of a good sales person include:

- energy and enthusiasm;
- basic intelligence and alertness;
- honesty and commitment;
- good communicator;

- good listener;
- likeable personality;
- good first impression;
- excellent IT skills;
- experience in sales;
- ability to cross-train.

These are all *subjective* values as opposed to measurable. It is assumed that you will ask your prospective salesperson for their last P60 to prove their earnings and their success and it is assumed their level of achieved sales in their last role can be confirmed without question.

The most important value in the list above is probably the most contentious. Customers buy from salespeople in small bites. In the first 30 seconds of meeting, they are likely to have assessed your sales person for handshake, eye contact, looks, style of clothes, cleanliness of shoes. They would have also made a subconscious decision as to the acceptability of body language, voice tone and smell.

Having passed the initial test of 30 seconds, your prospective customer will turn to the content of the opening discussion, which will take them to the two-minute mark. After two minutes, after passing the above test, your salesperson will have a further 10–20 minutes' discussion, to present the product, service or proposal and its value to the customer's business.

If your intrepid salesperson makes it passed the 20-minute watershed, then they are home and dry and are able to undertake exploratory discussions and suggest presentations or demonstrations, etc.

At any point during this initial meeting, your customer may make a subliminal or conscious decision that they simply do not warm to your salesperson. If this happens instant barriers raised will be raised, which will be very difficult to overcome. They will be obstacles to the sales discussion that follows and in some cases may result in the salesperson being instantly rejected as offering a credible solution.

This is the reaction of your customer, which needs no excuse, and no apology. When hiring a new salesperson this must be your reaction also. Listen to it, write it down and don't be ashamed to recognize it. If you feel uneasy, or just can't put your finger on it during the interview process, than it is absolutely certain your customer will feel the same. Listen to your instincts, as this individual will have a disproportionately high effect on your business' potential sales growth.

ACTIVE LISTENING

It is often said that selling is not about telling, is about listening.

The most common mistake that any salesperson can make and we will not exclude the business leader from this suggestion, is that there is not enough listening going on in the selling process.

There are many professional sales schools that will teach you how to actively listen, but this issue is so common we would like to present a small section dedicated to this skill. Feel free to use it in your own company as it is the development of this as a key sales skill that will help you for your quest to become a small business that lasts.

Communication with your customers is a two-way process. It is partly the things that you do that stimulate the senses of the person with whom you communicate, and partly how well your senses receive the messages that the other person transmits.

Most of the time, your 'receiving sensors' are your eyes and ears only. Yet people are notorious for failing to see things properly, and failing to hear what is said—as well as *how* it is said.

All too often, people use the 'gap' between their own bursts of speech to think of the next thing they want to say, rather than concentrating on what the other person is saying.

How to listen

As a mnemonic for your salespeople to learn, use the following well-known system:

L   Look interested
I   Inquire with questions

S   Stay on target

T   Test your understanding

E   Evaluate the message

N   Neutralise your feelings

driving sales

■ Look interested

Show encouragement by:

- facing the speaker;
- keeping eye contact;
- staying relaxed;
- leaning forward slightly;
- maintaining an open posture;
- trying not to fiddle or fidget.

■ Inquire with questions

- Clarify the speaker's meaning by using the 'If...then', form of questioning.
- Ensure you get the full story.
- Remember the various types of questions open to you—open ended, reflective and closed

■ Stay on target

- Stick to the point—remember your purpose and work to a written agenda which you can show your sales prospect.
- Listen for the central theme of what is being said and don't be in a rush to offer your product until you have heard from the customer the full extent of the problem.
- Think ahead but don't write down everything the customer says. It's annoying.
- Wait for the complete message. Don't prejudge your thoughts by making subjective judgements.
- Don't 'yes, but...'. Be patient and wait until the customer has completed their sentences.

■ **Test your understanding**

Ensure you really do understand what the speaker is saying. Restate if necessary to make sure, eg 'I So what you're saying is…'

Identify the speaker's purpose. Analyze what is said.

- Reasoning.
- Causes linked to effects?
- Emotional appeal?
- Facts or assertions?
- Complete or partial?
- Up-to-date? Reliable?
- Language.
- Use of unfamiliar words?
- Body language? Consistent with verbal message?
- Voice-related indicators?

■ **Neutralize your feelings**

- Stay calm: retain self control.
- Don't get heated or emotional.
- Keep an open mind.

L I S T E N—remember what it stands for!

CADENCE QUESTIONING

Selling isn't telling, it's asking questions

Information is the basis for the sale; knowledge of the facts, attitudes and opinions that relate to the selling situation.

This will tell you:

- whether the prospect will buy;
- what the prospect will buy;
- How you can sell

Types of questions

You are aware of the two basic types of questions:

- closed questions which elicit a 'Yes or No' answer, or a single piece of information;
- open ended questions which give you information in depth and an understanding of the prospect's attitudes and opinions.

Sharing the conversation

You should talk for only 40 per cent of the time in any sales situation. Effective questioning encourages your prospect to talk and leaves you free to listen, make notes, and consider the route to take in the rest of the meeting.

Controlling the conversation

Above all, questions enable you to control and direct the conversation. You must ensure that the direction of the conversation will lead you to the objectives you selected for the meeting.

Normally, salespeople think of a question that suits the situation at the time. Experienced salespeople have in their minds the 'standard' open ended questions they use regularly. Newer salespeople often have a note of those questions in their survey pad to help them. An interview should be a structured occasion designed to achieve your objectives by the finish. You cannot just leave to chance the order and direction of the 'signposts'—the questions that take you to your goal.

Cadence questioning is the use of a prepared *sequence* of questions designed to achieve an interview objective. These questions should be structured together. The technique is designed to move the prospect from thinking about the topic generally, to considering it in detail, and then concentrating on a significant benefit. Instead of 'snapshot' questions in random order, cadence questioning builds up your case for you.

In use, your questions could come one after the other. However, you usually explore one or two of the points brought up by the prospect's answers, before you move to the next prepared question in the cadence sequence.

The Cadence Sequence begins as follows.

1 *Background.*
   - What is the setting for the discussion?
   - Does the anticipated task or requirement exist?
   - Are the assumptions about the prospect correct?

2 *Implicit need.* Given that the situation is as you thought then there must be the general need that you expected to find. How is that handled at present? What is necessary to meet that need?

3 *Problem areas.* Now you can determine which particular aspects of the implicit need are the most sensitive, or significant, or vulnerable to the benefits you are able to offer.

4 *Problem development.*
   - What exactly is the significance to the prospect of the problem areas?
   - What is the cost, or loss?

5 *Explicit need.* Now you can determine the particular needs the prospect has been led to focus upon. Exactly what would the prospect want to change, or gain?

6 *Summary.* Summarize and confirm your understanding of the information you have been given.

7 *Check/question.* Always check in conclusion—is there anything else that has come to the prospect's mind while you have been summarizing?

8 *Problem and resolution.* Now you can match your offering—your benefits—to the explicit need outlined to you by the prospect.

Example: Using the cadence sequence

The prospect is a distributor for technical components. The company stocks a range of items, and dispatches them to the customers on receipt of phoned-in or written orders.

You have a system designed specifically for this application.

Example questions

These are just limited examples to indicate the trend of the discussion.

O indicates open ended questions. C indicates closed questions.

Background

O Tell me a little about how your business operates?

C How many live accounts do you have?

C How many people process orders?

C How many orders would you handle in a week?

O How effective do you believe the company is and why?

Moving closer to obtaining an order

The use of open and closed question in the form of cadence sequencing will give you the ability to structure your sales conversations. But conversations mean nothing without an order. So what steps do we need to take during the sales conversation, to bring our prospective customers closer to an order point?

There are many techniques that are available to a sales professional and we will now explore just three of what we consider the most valuable.

1 Use of trial closing.

2 Zip close technique.

3 Asking for the order.

■ Trial closes

Trial closing is the art of agreeing a point or even an order by way of suggestion. It evolves around the use of 'if' and 'then'.

Example: If I could provide you with a product in blue as opposed to red, does this meet your need?

Trial closing is a very common objection handling technique but a very powerful one that is often underused.

Try it for yourself.

'If the price were acceptable then would you place an order?' A trial close statement which strips away the price from your negotiation and allows you to focus instead upon the product and its features.

The prospect may have used price as the objection when what he really wanted was a change to your product specification, which he didn't make clear to you.

Using if, then statements, it is possible to break down your proposal into many component parts identifying the real cause of the customer's objection or the real opportunity to solve a problem.

It's like a selling a car, for example. The customer is hesitating and you use the if, then trial technique to identify the real objection/s.

Example: If the price was right Sir, and the service history available, if we could get the colour you wanted and if the specification met your needs, then would you purchase the vehicle? The prospect hesitates for a moment and then says no, because what I need is a left hand

Using the if, then technique, you proposed in your opinion the ideal solution and yet when handled in this way, the customer eventually gave you the real reason and their objection.

Try it for fun! If I mow the lawn and wash the car then can I read my newspaper? It's amazing how often if, then statements are accepted as a fair way of negotiating.

We are now going to take this a stage further.

◼ Zip close technique

This is a combination of the 'if, then' technique and cadence questioning sequence.
Narrowing your conversation down, using open questioning to establish as much background and information as possible, you will start to focus on a specific solution or application on which to base your sale. Your discussions will start to become a mix of less open and more closed questions. Closed questions, remember, have specific answers.

Taking the close questions and applying the if, then technique it should be possible to achieve a zip close.

So what is a zip close? It is the simple bringing together of the prospect and the solution, step by step, closing as you go, just like a zip. Occasionally you may revert to open questions, to discuss objections, but a zip close is based upon an increasing frequency of closed questions. Let's try it....

Example:

C= Closed Question	O = Open Question

(Customer dialogue is shown in bold)

You are trying to sell a lathe to a manufacturing director in a small company. You have discussed his specific needs and specification of your product in a previous meeting, and you have taken the opportunity to arrange this meeting believing your prospect to be in the closed cycle, ie about to make a decision. Your prospect objects to the price and the conversation might go along like this

I like your product, but the price is too high.

If the price could be adjusted to meet your needs, would you be able to place an order? (C)

I'm not sure, I will have to think about it.

If price was put to one side, then could you tell me what else is concerning you? (O)

It's just that the operators don't know your machines as well as those of your competitors.

Can you be exact as to the features or operations that are different or not explained correctly? (O)

The shop floor just loves the auto-adjuster feature and doesn't want to lose it.

If the auto-adjuster feature were available on our model, then would you select our solution? (C)

Yes I would, as long as we understood how it worked. ▶

driving sales

> If I were to offer free training and the price stays the same, then can you place your order with us? (C)
>
> **Yes, I believe I can.**

In the above role-play, price was not a problem for the buyer at all; it came down to identifying an important feature, which has not been completely explained by the sales person. The sales person reacted well and not only offered a solution in terms of the feature being available, but also overcame any lingering doubts, by offering the customer free training. He would not have to reduce his price, as he removed it from the conversation earlier, using his if, then statements. When he brought price back into the conversation, it was not cited as a problem and he didn't have to reduce his order value.

We now move to the last stage in effective selling.

■ Asking for the order

It is quite amazing how often, we see perfectly professional, experienced salespeople, who articulate their words well and are seen to be successful, yet for some reason find it difficult to ask for the order.

It is somehow seen as confrontational or rude, yet asking for the order at the right time, is critical if you are not going to take one meeting too many and start to lose the confidence of your prospect.

Just the simple words, 'Can I have your order please?' sometimes strikes fear into the hearts of some salespeople. This is of course the fear of rejection.

'Can I have the order please?.....' 'No'. Doesn't exactly leave the salesperson in a strong position. However, using cadence questioning sequence and the 'if, then' qualifying close, it should be possible to arrive safely, with a soft landing, and with nobody getting hurt, when the question 'Can I have the order please' is popped!

There are of course, many ways of asking for the order, without being so blunt. It is a question of style and market place.

In professional circles, we often use phrases like 'Can I now draw up the contracts' or 'when can you issue me with a purchase number?' A softer close could be 'Can I sort the paperwork out?' The approach is down to you or your salesperson as sales is all about enthusiasm and personality.

If you do not ask for the order, the customer is compelled to come to you with an offer of an order. This starts to undermine the feelings of confidence in your company and the feeling that they are about to be looked after in the delivery process.

> Placing an order for the customer is when they enter a time of heightened risk; they are committing their company's money to a project for which they are responsible, and they naturally feel exposed. Will they be let down, will you deliver as per your promises, will they experience difficulties or problems they are not in control of, will their internal reputation be affected by placing this order with you?

In the 1980s, IBM summed up the situation very well, in the now very famous saying 'No-one ever gets fired for buying from IBM'.

To finish this chapter, let us examine the period immediately after you have received the purchase order from your customer.

This is a high-risk time for you and your company, despite having won the order. The buyer has a tendency of going through a period of 'buyer's remorse'. This manifests as a series of questions, worries or doubts in the buyer's mind, particularly if this is his first dealing with your company. It is essential, that you the salesperson retains regular contact immediately after the order has been won, to reduce buyer's remorse.

You may have to remind your customer, as to all the good reasons why he has placed his order with you and in some ways resell the solution to him or his colleagues.

The process of driving sales is the hardest to get right in any small business. For a small business built to last, we must concentrate on identifying real customers and managing the selling process to them as effectively as possible. Selling is a matter of style and it is an art form. However, there are basic rules and given processes that turn an artistic sales person into a professional one.

Your business built to last will undergo product transformation and even customer type transformation and the skills of your team, and including yourself as a business leader must be regularly refreshed and updated if you are to succeed.

BUILDING BLOCK 9

- Analyze and plot your base business by using RCM and 90-day development plans.

- Plot your development business and use the Action Plan (Form 3).

- Understand your business sales and continually compare with sales budget.

- Accurately plan for extra/fewer staff depending upon real numbers.

- Qualify your prospects using the questionnaire and other sales measurements regularly.

- Understand the attributes of sales staff and recruit accordingly.

- Ensure all sales staff are trained in active listening techniques.

- Ensure your sales staff are trained in controlling and directing the conversation by using the cadence sequence.

- Use the zip close technique, 'if and then' statements to ask for the order.

- Reduce 'buyer's remorse' and contact your customers regularly after the order has been won.

- The rapid change management process can help in right-sizing and expansion of your business.

10

market masters

Organizational energy

Recruitment strategy

Staff retention

Organizational theory

Steps to take when designing
an organization

The role of the leader

Optimism is that highly contagious emotion that when shared with one or two people creates an automatic uplift in both intellect, productivity and energy levels

Having arrived at the final chapter of this book, you, the business leader will have identified that building a business to last is not a process or a destination, it is actually a journey.

Part 1 of the book covered the preparation required and the thought processes needed in order for you to plan your journey. We then moved on to Part 2, a fitter more focused business and set about learning the environment of e-business, how to identify real customers and partnering in the market place. These three chapters took our leaner more focused business and gave it the tools to become more competitive in the market place of tomorrow. In this final section, we have taken the subjects covered and applied them in a practical, and results orientated way.

This application has now provided you with the skills not just as a leader, but as a company to manage rapid change, manage and contain the associated risks and take a positive step forward in reaching out to the market, instead of waiting for it to arrive.

Your journey has not come to an end however, it is simply beginning. The focus of Market Masters is to develop organizational energy that will be self sustaining and enduring as your journey continues.

ORGANIZATIONAL ENERGY

What is organizational energy?

If you recall, in the opening chapters we suggested that two similar businesses in two adjacent towns servicing similar customers with identical products at the same price would only differentiate themselves from one another by their people and their teams.

If you accept this principle, then the type of people, their energy and enthusiasm, combined with the way the business leader organizes and manages them, is a key differentiator in the small business for the future.

Building a small business to last relies heavily upon the fact that you have excellent and enthusiastic people who work consistently in the business over a great period of time. We have already discussed in Chapter 9 *Driving sales* some of the key attributes of a sales person and we explored in our rightsizing section in Chapter 4 *Embracing the risks* some of the key characteristics that you would positively retain in your business.

Building from both of these chapters, we find a common picture of enthusiasm, commitment, intellect, IT skills, etc.

Three aspects we have not explored in detail so far are their ability to be entrepreneurial when the situation calls, and the ability to step outside of their own role in pursuit of an outcome. The third aspect that we would like you to look out for in all of your existing and new staff is optimism. Optimism is that highly contagious emotion that when shared with one or two people creates an automatic uplift in both intellect, productivity and energy levels.

Recruiting people for your small business is one of the most essential tasks that you the business leader can stay involved in for a long time to come. Until you get to a meaningful size, every employee or team member will make a significant impact in your business.

Do not delegate the role of hiring simply because it is a time-consuming task or you believe it is an unimportant task.

Remember in Chapter 4 *Embracing the risks* that we suggested the business leader should spend time ensuring that the core group of original team members does not alienate or cause barriers to exist when new members arrive. If this happens your business will have negative energy flowing within it which is contrary to your business goals.

In Chapter 9 *Driving sales*, we agreed that 'first impressions' count with salespeople. We set out a theoretical time scale in which your customers will judge acceptance or non acceptance of your sales person based upon their person, body language, voice tone, etc. To a lesser extent but still relevant, this applies with all of your recruitment as with non-sales recruitment.

In our businesses we ran recruitment panels, consisting of three people from the business taking time out to interview the final stage. In this way, first impression can be accounted for across the team and not just by yourself. By including other team members you will always generate an earlier acceptance of a new team member as it has become a collective decision.

RECRUITMENT STRATEGY

The most important thing about your team members is the ability they have to cross-train to other functions and competencies. Even though skills are important, a highly motivated individual who is keen to learn can develop the skills sought by you in future changes to your business.

There can be too much emphasis on applicants' skills rather than their ability to cross-train effectively into other areas of competencies. This should be considered by the business leader. As we have already expressed in earlier chapters, enthusiasm, energy, motivation and intellectual alertness are all key characteristics of good employees.

Growth in the use of the Internet is revolutionizing the way the recruitment for certain roles is taking place. Recent research has suggested that 25 per cent of 34–42 year olds suggest that they will use the Internet as well as traditional means to find their next job. In industry, according to the Chartered Institute of Personnel and Development, 40 per cent of organizations are now using one or more forms of electronic media in their recruitment and selection.

For professionals on the other hand, the trade press is the most common route to finding their next role, but amongst manual workers, job centres and newspapers are the main route to finding a job.

So how does a small business search and select the very best candidates available in the market?

market masters

This very much depends on the role, salary and seniority of the candidate. Experienced business managers are likely to advertise themselves for a job on the website. Rather they would contact senior recruitment consultants or head hunters to secure their next role. Similarly, manual workers are less likely to have access to the Internet and therefore will revert to the old tried and tested job centres. You must target whatever media is appropriate in order to track the best selection of candidates to your company. Some of these methods are more expensive than others, but don't forget the use of your own website and local newspaper editorial which is often free, and can be an excellent and cost effective way to attract staff.

Once you have identified a potential new recruit, you should give consideration as to how you will go about testing the candidate and ensuring a good team fit. By far the most common is the interview process with 99.6 per cent of companies using this technique for selection. Personality questionnaires would be used in conjunction with the interview with 36.3 per cent of employees. Ability tests would be employed by 54.2 per cent of employees with less tangible techniques such as bio-data and graphology accounting for only 8.8 per cent (source: CIPD).

Interviewing can be a fallible process as it is often the case that the business leader has not undertaken formal skill training to conduct interviews. The interviewer must carefully plan questions, which are designed to entice candidates into providing critical detailed and sometimes personal information. An interview should not be allowed to degenerate into a chat about the applicant's hobbies or unrelated history.

When interviewing, the business leader must be aware of the strategic purpose of the business and subordinate any prejudices or preferences. It is commonly agreed that business leaders generally recruit in their own image but overriding this should be a desire to hire someone who is better than yourself for the position you are recruiting.

We strongly suggest that your employment contracts are revised regularly by your lawyer to ensure compliance with latest employment legislation. Always provide the company with a three-month probationary clause to the new recruit, during which time both parties can separate with no obligations. This will act as your safety net if the decision to employ a candidate turns out badly for either party. See *Small*

Business Handbook (Webb and Webb, Prentice Hall 2001) containing a CD-ROM which provides a comprehensive, set of relevant forms and review techniques to UK Investors In People standard.

STAFF RETENTION

Earlier we stated that retention of key individuals or 'business jewel' as we have previously referred to them, is highly desirable when building a business to last. There are few things more disruptive to a small business than to lose a good team member unnecessarily. It is this that the business leader must plan to avoid wherever possible.

Staff retention can be a complicated subject in itself, and at the end of the day can come down to a large number of intangibles. Team members stay within the business for many different reasons. The obvious reason is of course for salary, but you would be surprised at how few people would stay in a business where they were unhappy just for the pay. Using the rapid change management techniques described in Chapter 8 *Rapid change management*, it is possible to understand the collective feelings of your team from time to time. Simply by running an RCM session, with the question, *'what can we do to make this the best company ever?'*, then the planning issues received on the anonymous form 1s will tell you how your team feels. Most key people in an organization yearn for a sense of belonging and a sense of fair play. Salary is important but certainly not top of the list for many.

Personal development, ie the ability to learn and develop as an individual is often one of the key reasons for working for a small business. It is important to note that this does not have to be by formal external courses. It can simply be the ability to move between roles, experience different situations and be entrusted with disparate responsibilities.

As entrepreneurship becomes acceptable and even desirable, compared to say 20 years ago, shared risk and shared reward are things that the business leader must consider with the team. Does your company allow employee shared ownership for example? Or have you considered issuing share options for little cost? The use of equity-linked benefits can be a very powerful motivational instrument, which can bind a small team with a sense of common purpose and shared rewards.

Equity instruments

The term 'equity' relates to shareholding structures of your company, as mentioned in the Finance and accounting section of Chapter 8 *Rapid change management*, as a small business, unless you have raised additional money through shares, your share capital will probably be set at just £100.

Depending on your position you may wish to allow existing and future employees to purchase shares in your business thereby expanding the capital base of your company and creating extremely strong links with your employees. This action would support our premise that the small business built to last must strive for a low turnover of staff.

Methods of offering shares will vary from company to company, but you can 'sell' your company to a 'new holding company' in exchange for say 75 per cent of the shares in the new holding company (Inland Revenue Tax Clearance is required before you do this) to avoid a tax charge.

Then you are able to offer the 25 per cent balance as available shares to purchase. The price of these shares is under your control and so you are not being asked to give away one per cent for one pound as in your original share structure.

Clearly if you are not trading your company's shares on the stock market then the ability of your employees to sell these shares will be limited.

Your team will therefore be focused upon building up shareholder value in anticipation of a future flotation or trade sale from which they can profit.

If the above suggestion of offering shares to individuals is not palatable, and there are many reasons why you might not want to distribute the shares in your company, then a mechanism known as a *share option* can be equally effective.

There are many schemes available and you should consult your accountant for advice. Essentially, you will issue the employee with a document giving them the right to purchase shares from you at an agreed price that is set from the outset. The conditions by which these share options can be converted to shares for payment can be established and agreed up front.

For example, a time limit of not earlier than three years may be your preference, or a statement relating to performance of either the company or the individual may become the trigger point. Once the option becomes triggerable, then the holder must pay over the price of the share that was agreed at the outset. If the business has moved on and expanded, then the share price on the day will be deemed to be higher, and the option holder has achieved a paper profit.

If, however, the business has experienced negative factors since the option was granted, then it may well be that the on-the-day price is lower that the option price. Clearly, the option would not be exercised if this were the case, and the employee may feel disenchanted or excluded. This was the case for many of the dot.com employees in late 1999/2000, when company values fell so dramatically that the option prices were far in excess of the tradable shares. Employees had the wrong end of the deal and the motivational good will was lost.

Using this as a sensible instrument, however, it is possible to drive the collective team towards a common financial goal designed to trigger a disposal situation. This can be a very powerful tool in the armoury of the Business Leader and provide an exciting and sustainable motivator for the team over time.

Consult your accountant or solicitor for further details of the various applicable schemes that are available to your business. It is no longer safe to assume that key workers are satisfied to work for a small business owner with no prospect of shared reward. As times change, then we must consider all aspects of retention, and take a hard look at collective equity participation as a tool for building our business to last.

Alternative packages

There are many alternative options open to the business owner who wishes to create an environment for staff retention. This is largely a matter for the individual company when it comes to creating menus of benefits, such as pension, health, childcare, other expenses, etc.

However, one powerful alternative to shares or share options is to link the performance of your business directly to the reward of your employee. To do this, the measurement of your business must be exact and not subjective. Individual performance can form part of a separate link to remuneration. The company must be prepared to offer a link to the net profitability of the operation, as long as your team have collective responsibilities for expenditure and it is never the case that profit suppressing expenditure is made which would run contrary to fair play.

There are many pitfalls associated with net profit bonus schemes. One of these may be to lead to a temptation to suppress investment in order to save money, so as to increase profit and thereby increase bonuses. However, be creative in your approach and see if your business and its operation would support such a scheme.

Recruitment of key staff can often be a very expensive process, with some agencies asking for 25 per cent of the employee's starting salary as a fee. In addition to this cost is the impact of the time that is consumed by you and your team during the recruitment process, interviewing, reviewing, planning etc and after the team member joins in training, induction and reviewing.

These costs are sometimes viewed as dead money. It can never be recovered, nor does the time or money that you put into the recruitment process make your eventual candidate any better than they are already. Looked at from another perspective, however, the interview can be seen as an opportunity to learn about:

- products;
- companies;
- customers;
- pricing;
- suppliers;
- level of sales in different market sectors and companies;
- marketing concepts;
- use of IT etc.

In addition, the induction process need not be time consuming if your existing staff have a two-way conversation with the new team member and based on their previous experiences, learn about different processes, ways of doing things and approaches, which may make your business more efficient than it is today.

The choice is entirely yours as to which way you review the recruitment process, but on the basis that the process is largely the same whatever you think, we will encourage you to adopt the more optimistic option.

ORGANIZATIONAL THEORY

At the beginning of this chapter we introduced the concept of organizational energy and decided that this energy comes from the people who make up the team.

So far we have covered recruiting of people, the search for optimism and the need to retain key staff. All of these are relevant as we as business leaders attempt to drive up our organizational levels.

Imagine a pile of batteries in the middle of a room. Each of these batteries is a 1.5-volt, long-life battery. They are all capable of powering the pocket torch that you carry around with you and what a long time your pocket torch can be lit for. However, if you take all of these batteries individually, and connect them end-to-end, in a positive negative system, then and only then, will you reap the benefits of the collective effect of all the batteries.

The same thing happens in your business. The way in which your people connect to each other is directly proportional to the organizational energy to your business. In this next section you will discover how to organize your team in your business to derive the maximum energy and create the most efficient small business that is built to last.

For the last 100 years, industrialists have developed many thought processes which are published as management theory on how to manage workers. We use the term 'workers' because most of the theories on developing management teams and span of control come from the industrial age.

In the late 1980s and early 1990s, huge numbers of middle-managers were culled from the world's industrial organizations in a desperate bid to reduce costs, free up information and make the general workforce more responsive and in touch with the way the company wanted to run.

The scenario above describing connecting batteries in series is particular valid when describing the organizational structure of a company. If, for example, you connected one of your batteries incorrectly in the long chain of batteries, then it would have the effect of cancelling the power of the battery next to it. In the same way, if you connect conflicting team members or business processes the disruptive element is likely to increase workload, increase confusion and reduce optimism.

Recent theorists discuss flat management structures and this is fine for those who run large businesses. If you have a small operation, then you may have no report lines at all but you still have an organizational structure. How do we organize the structure in our business correctly?

In your mind, do two things.

1   Separate the management report lines, ie who manages who, from the organization of the company, ie who performs which role.

2   Define the organization in terms of the functions and roles that it performs (do not think about individual people in these roles).

The next step is to write these down and record, probably with your team's help, all of the roles, tasks and functions within your business.

When you have completed this, you then have to define the work that your business does each and every day. To help you action this list, which is easy when you get started but difficult to start, we have suggested some areas on which you can base your own list. See Figure 10.1 and then move on to completing Form 4, Organization Analysis (see Figure 10.2), to complete your personal organization structure.

BUSINESS DEVELOPMENT

Market research

Government relations

Product development:
- laboratory
- technical
- acquisition
- research.

Market development:
- task force
- field teams
- research
- promotion.

Diversification and acquisition

Business planning and investment

Analysis

Product design

Process & equipment R&D and design

PRODUCTION OR PROCESS

Sales order processing

Shop release

Process order control

Production supervision

Inventory control

Stores and stock control

Production control and planning

Quality control, inspection and quality
assurance

Tooling and tooling stores

Industrial engineering

Manpower planning

Facilities planning

Time and motion standards and methods

Product field service

Maintenance

Warehouse and depot

Transport and materials handling

Receiving and inspection

PURCHASING

Plant, equipment, transport – purchasing

Materials purchasing

Value engineering and Vendor/supplier
qualification

Subcontract administration

Contract administration

Receiving and inspection

Pilot production shops

Make or buy analysis

Lease or buy analysis

Purchase bid preparation, negotiations,
award

Engineering changes negotiations

Change board operations

SALES AND MARKETING

Sales order administration

Sales statistics:
- Ration sales to employee by skills
- force level forecasting
- consumer statistics
- consumption statistics
- quotas
- calls, costs, closure and capture rates
- win or lose statistics.

Direct mail selling

Direct field force selling

Salary and incentive programmes

Missionary selling

Sales training

Public relations and advertising

Customer service and customer training

Sales aids and point of sale support

Demonstrations and exhibitions

Presentations and seminars and
conferences

Audio-visuals

TECHNICAL SERVICE

Estimating and quotations

Customer contract administration, warranties and insurance

Design engineering liaison… customer and supplier

Service administration:

- repair
- investigation
- depot and transport.

On-site customer support:

- subcontract management to customer
- resident technical assistance

DISTRIBUTION

Warehouse, depot, transport

Administration-subcontract and evaluation

Packing and shipping-containerization

Insurance

Customer receiving and inspection

ACCOUNTING AND FINANCE

Sales and credit control

Cash and banking relations—financial

Planning and management

Shareholder relations

Debtors, creditors

Computer operations and management information systems

Tax administration

Legal administration

Pricing and discounts and warranties, Terms of sale

Leasing and financing

Investment management, portfolios

Retirement, subsidiaries

Audit

PERSONNEL AND MANAGEMENT

Training

Recruiting, testing, and evaluation

Performance evaluation

Management development

Incentives and motivation systems

Wage and salary administration

Labour relations

Site, community public relations

Employee social activities

Social environment and amenities

Safety, security

Organization development

Corporate planning

Strategy and strategic management

Career path planning

Consultant evaluation and qualification

Management systems evaluation

INFORMATION TECHNOLOGY

Business analysis

Systems analysis

Software architecture

Systems designing

Software engineering

Hardware engineering

Systems engineering

Help desk operations

Website designing

Website programming

Application programming

Database programming

Specialist programming

Fig.10.1 ▪ **Checklist for functions and elements in organisation design**

STEPS TO TAKE WHEN DESIGNING AN ORGANIZATON

Having established the workload and the tasks performed in your business it is now time to apply the cash flow test.

Here's the question. What is the impact of the role, function or task upon generating positive cash flow for your business?

Look at the words carefully. The word 'generating' will dispel any confusion about cost savings or efficiencies as this is about generating positive cash flow.

Next work through the following task sheet and generate for yourself an Organization Analysis Form (Form 4) as shown below.

1 Name the organization. Classify the working purpose of the organization by carefully naming the operations. The names should be guided by the 'end use' of the product or services being offered.

2 Identify all of the individual functions and work elements required to make up the whole of the operational activity. This includes the day-to-day work as well as the developmental activities. List each function one over the other down the left side of the page.

3 Rank each of these functional elements by assigning either a level 1 (most important) level 2 (medium importance) or level 3 (low importance). On the right side of the page make three columns (see Figure 10.2). Column 1 on the far right, followed by Column 2; with Column 3 nearest to the list of functional work elements. Insert an appropriate column as to the impact on generating positive cash flow.

4 Rotate the page to landscape.

5 All of the functions that have a tick at the top ie, in the No. 1 column must command the undelegated attention of the business leader. If your organization is larger, then ensure all of the functions with a tick in the No.2 column are signed to competent managers.

6 Group like elements into families of like work. Give each group a name. Separate operational work from developmental work.

7 Conduct a 'make or buy' analysis on each function shown on the

chart, to determine if the function should be purchased, on a sub-contract basis, or 'socialized'. Socialized means to keep within the organization, using employees hired for that purpose. Keep all functions where the technology is key to the product function.

8   Establish a 'workload' ratio for each function ie, distribute the work fairly within your business.

9   Establish 'direct to indirect' relationships for support functions. Force fit to industrial norms. Examples: inside sales staff to field sales staff; inspectors to workers; industrial engineers to shop floor personnel.

10   Lay out a draft organization structure. Calculate for each function the numbers of people required to support your sales forecast.

11   Calculate the salary and wage expense for the organization and check these costs against the profit and loss forecast. Reiterate the calculations, making changes to fit a realistic approach to managing the business. Get the right loadings through this trial and error (cut to fit) approach.

The Organization Analysis Form (Figure 10.2) has shown you that by grouping the tasks of the business into like work, you are able to assign this work to the business by defining its relationship to positive cash flow.

You may have been surprised to discover that some of the work that you, as business leader, do on a daily basis may have nothing to do with generating positive cash flow. Conversely you may also discover that cash-generating tasks are being currently handled by your team members who may or may not be qualified to manage this.

Use the Organization Analysis Form (Figure 10.2) to connect up your batteries within your company. Involve your team in this activity to make sure that no batteries are connected incorrectly.

Understand the impact of development work and the additional work flow this may cause to you and your team. You have now completed the organization analysis and will, we hope, use this exercise to understand the importance of your cash generative functions and then you will have connected your batteries to provide your business with the maximum organizational energy.

ORGANIZATION ANALYSIS (Form 4)

	(column 3)	(column 2)	(column 1)
Task or role within the business	Low (3)	Mid (2)	High (1)
Wage and salary administration	•		
Direct field force selling			•
Terms of business and pricing strategy			•
Training of management		•	
Tax planning			•
Help desk operations	•		

Note: *Examples are inserted to illustrate the use of the form.*

Fig. 10.2

Analyze your organization periodically to maintain a constant focus on cash generation, and upon a fair distribution of work within your team. This periodical analysis can be used to offer different or development work to your team members providing opportunities to cross train and to maintain a high level of enthusiasm, learning interest and optimism.

The benefits of your organizational review can be summarised as follows:

- constant focus on cash generation—keep the business mean
- cross-training of team members—keep the business robust
- don't hire, reassign work—keep the business lean
- maintain operational optimism—keep the team members keen
- install IT wherever possible—keep the business competitive

THE ROLE OF THE LEADER

As we come to this last section, the corner stone to becoming a market master in a 21st Century business, is you the business leader. Because it is your decisions, your actions and your attitude that will ultimately determine whether you are a casualty of the competition or whether you will build a business that will truly last.

The 20th Century witnessed phenomenal changes in infrastructure, industrialisation, manufacturing and development of IT. In the 21st Century, the material developments will continue but at a much greater pace and with bigger changes in the way in which we communicate, and the way we amass information. Technology convergence is unstoppable and will affect everybody in business today at some point. It is your role as a 21st Century business leader to accept this challenge and to be crowned a market master.

The dynamics of business in this new century will be that small business in having a level playing field with larger businesses in terms of technology availability and Internet marketing ability will be forced to be compete on infrastructure grounds as well.

What do we mean?

The international large corporation—with whom you are now able to compete with website presence and speed on low-cost products to market by using partnerships— has a global presence. It is this global presence which you are competing against and you have to engage in the fight for the customer.

Your small business will be driven at a rate depending on your market sector into a 24-hour operation. For a retainer of less than £50 per month, using effective technology you are able to accept telephone calls from your customers, 24 hours a day, 7 days a week. Call centres offering this service are becoming common and coupled with the ability to transfer calls from a call centre to anywhere in the world, land-based or mobile, your business will have to start to assume a different shape in the future.

Automation of your business processes and your business responses certainly to its customers and suppliers is a key to becoming a market master. Automation means using effective low-cost available IT and it is your job as the business leader to seek it out. Do not benchmark your business against competition and believe that you are maintaining your position—remember the example of Boeing and the way it consumed Douglas with the adoption of the jet engine for commercial flying. You have to look for the unobvious, the hidden and the converging, spot the trend, adopt the technology, automate the business and master your market.

Your role in business leadership must be focused upon your own personal development. Unless you continually educate yourself, the opportunity and the clues will pass you by. Use every opportunity to learn, whether through formal training courses, seminars or simply an invitation to network with a different type of business. It is this diversity of outlooks that you need to assume if you are to concentrate your mind on finding new markets, developing new products, cultivating successful partnerships and embracing e-business, and undertaking the task of finding real customers and locking them into your business. Base your actions upon facts, not reactions. Don't settle for anything but the best, as your customers certainly won't. When you have found a real customer, nurture them, look after them and create the opportunities to use the mechanisms that bind them to you.

If you do this well, these customers will allow you to develop a business that is profitable and sustainable. Do it poorly and you will be constantly in search of new customers at a huge cost.

Your innovation and intellect will separate you from your competitors. It will generate a need from your customers for your service and products.

As a business leader you must switch on the optimism of your team and by joining the batteries of their abilities then you will connect the energy of the organization to the task at hand. You must at all costs maintain organizational energy by hiring the best people, allowing them to assume different responsibilities and constantly reviewing the organization, its tasks, responsibilities and opportunities to alternate. It is your people at the end of the day, who—inspired by your leadership and your sense of fair play—will use their optimistic energy to ensure the business success.

Avoid the fear of change by adopting rapid change management concepts and sharing its operation with your team. The team, through its optimistic energy, will then embrace change as a culture as opposed to a task and the resultant excitement and quest for newnesss will maintain your business as a forerunner in your market.

The attributes of a business leader who becomes a market master may be debated for a long time. Market masters are not super heroes—they are people like you and me with positive attitude.

It is this positive attitude that delivers education, fair play, constant newness and inclusive culture when it comes to rewards, plus an energy level that is contagious.

If there are to be only three things that you, the market master will concentrate on in order to achieve the above, you might consider the following.

- **Plan for the future**—unless you decide which road to take, then any road will get you there! It is this ability and willingness to plan that will enable you to identify opportunities, spot difficulties, and to build a robust attention to cash generative activities. Use short-term, 90-day written-down development plans for rapid change recognition.

■ **Continued training of yourself**—stale or copied ideas never made a business great so you must continually train and educate to ensure newness of ideas and understanding of technology in a constantly developing outlook on behalf of your customers.

■ **Constant focus upon purchasing**—keeping your business 'lean and mean'; a focus upon containment of cash will ensure that your business is built on solid foundations.

Becoming a market master is not an end result, it is part of life's journey. Small businesses in the 21st Century will be faster moving and more exciting than in the last century. For those business leaders who do not aspire to be market masters, then the going will be tough. Markets in the 21st Century will be identifiable by all the attributes listed above; we hope that by constant reference to this book, we have helped you to achieve a map for your journey. Your business can be unique and exciting. With constant change as its companion and real customers as its friends, then the outcome surely has to be a small business built to last.

BUILDING BLOCK 10

■ **Build organizational energy in the business through the recruitment of highly enthused, committed individuals.**

■ **Do not delegate the role of recruitment.**

■ **Organize recruitment panels to ensure that first impressions are a collective decision.**

■ **Recruit team members who have the ability to cross-train to other functions and competencies to ensure your business can move forward into competitive markets.**

■ **Advertise your vacancies on the Internet.**

■ **Carefully plan interview questions and use the interview process to understand the market place, competitor awareness and market trends.**

- Ensure your employment contracts are compliant with the latest employment legislation.

- Consider the retention of key individuals as your 'business jewels'.

- Use equity linked benefits to retain key staff and as a powerful motivational instrument.

- Use Form 4 and analyze the roles, tasks and functions within your business.

- As a business leader, focus on your own personal development and educate yourself whenever the opportunity arises.

- Plan for the future every quarter with 90-day development plans.

- Focus on the containment of cash in your business.

- Remember, market masters are not super heroes, they are people like you and me, with positive attitude!

THE BUILDING BLOCKS TO SUCCESS

BLOCK 10

- Build organizational energy in the business through the recruitment of highly enthused, committed individuals.
- Do not delegate the role of recruitment.
- Organize recruitment panels to ensure that first impressions are a collective decision.
- Recruit team members who have the ability to cross-train to other functions and competencies to ensure your business can move forward into competitive markets.
- Advertise your vacancies on the Internet.
- Carefully plan interview questions and use the interview process to understand the market place, competitor awareness and market trends.
- Ensure your employment contracts are compliant with the latest employment legislation.
- Consider the retention of key individuals as your 'business jewels'.
- Use equity linked benefits to retain key staff and as a powerful motivational instrument.
- Use Form 4 and analyze the roles, tasks and functions within your business.
- As a business leader, focus on your own personal development and educate yourself whenever the opportunity arises.
- Plan for the future every quarter with 90-day development plans.
- Focus on the containment of cash in your business.
- Remember, Market Masters are not super heroes, they are people like you and me, with positive attitude!

BLOCK 7

- Building partners in the market offers a number of advantages, such as increase in salesforce, joint marketing initiatives, joint customer bases and increased key customers.
- Select the right partners through product analysis, geography and adding value.
- Formulate a market vision with your new partner.
- Measure the partnership to see if it is a successful alliance.
- Connect IT and 'affinity link' with your partner's website.
- Ensure you have adequate virus protection/system security in place.
- Syndicate your alliances on the Internet to the virtual world.
- Identify appropriate market acquisitions to make long lasting alliances, which will add to your competitive edge.
- Consult a solicitor and understand the cost and steps that will be involved in your acquisition.
- Make sure there is a cultural fit as this is the biggest single cause of failure in acquisitions.

BLOCK 8

How to manage change in your business

- Prepare:
  - The RCM committee defines the problem area;
  - a team leader and executive team are appointed to carry out the RCM procedure;
  - all employees with a contribution to make send in their views to the team.

  Planning Issue Form 1 required.
- RCM workshop:
  - the team sorts the views and makes preliminary recommendations;
  - the team refines and reviews the recommendations;
  - the leader obtains a team commitment to the recommendations.

  Recommended Action Form 2 required.
  - Presentation.
  - Agreed actions are proposed to the Managing Director for approval.

  Action Plan Form 3 required.
- Get results:
  - the MD approves actions after alteration, if necessary;
- Control:
  - after an agreed interval, the team assembles to control and assess progress and initiate corrective actions if required.
- Understanding the finance and accounting in your business will ensure you can plan and forecast your business accurately.
- Study your management accounts regularly.
- Train and develop your knowledge on all matters of finance in the business.

BLOCK 9

- Analyze and plot your base business by using RCM and 90-day development plans.
- Plot your development business and use the Action Plan (Form 3).
- Understand your business sales and continually compare with sales budget. Accurately plan for extra/fewer staff depending real numbers.
- Qualify your prospects using the questionnaire and other sales measurements regularly.
- Understand the attributes of sales staff and recruit accordingly.
- Ensure all sales staff are trained in active listening techniques.
- Ensure your sales staff are trained in controlling and directing the conversation by using the cadence sequence.
- Use the zip close technique, if and then statements to ask for the order.
- Reduce 'buyer's remorse' and contact your customers regularly after the order has been won.
- The rapid change management process can help in right-sizing and expansion of your business.

BLOCK 6

- Remember that 80 per cent of the value in your customer base comes from just 20 per cent of the customers.
- The ability to sell to an existing customer is far less expensive that the operation to find a new one.
- Hold information on all of your customers to find your real customers.
- Use IT to be part of your customer's operation.
- Understand your good customers and lock them into your business.
- Seek out repeat earnings potential from your customers.
- Offer varied finance tools to your customers.
- Increase your order value by examining how you bundle products or services together.
- Form partnerships with your real customers.
- Share strategic plans with your customer.

BLOCK 1

- Understand the world is changing at an ever-faster pace over which you have little control.
- Make decisions and develop a willingness to move out of your comfort zone.
- Understand each decision has a consequence and a new direction.
- Your continued development and training is essential for your business success.
- Embrace new technologies and innovate.
- Challenge your thought processes and business rationale regularly.
- Glass ceilings are there to be broken.
- Take all of the above and disseminate it to your staff.

BLOCK 5

- Business to business growth on the Internet is much faster than business to customer on the Internet. However, business to consumer services will increase significantly over the next 10 years.
- The key word for small business is *automation* to increase competitiveness.
- Embrace the technologies and the e-business models. Adopt IT- led changes and connect to all your partners/customers/suppliers where appropriate.
- E-mail will reduce costs and allow your business to adopt a speed that you would never achieve without it.
- As a supplier to your customer, the ability to send electronic notes or attach pictures or complex files within minutes has become a necessity and not a luxury.
- By opening a website on the World Wide Web, your business is automatically international. It can sell and update existing and new customers, link up with suppliers and sell via partners/distributors. All net business documents can be accessed remotely away from the office.
- If you shy away from e-business, then a gradual decline and erosion of your business will be seen in the years to follow.
- Challenge the Internet and reach out for the knowledge. It's only a machine connected to a telephone line and you cannot break it.
- Show willingness to be open and to share information with your team, customers, suppliers and partners to truly affect profitability.
- Too much internal focus or too little could create more processes and paperwork and cause impaired performance/little savings.

BLOCK 2

- Understand your market place and ensure that your business planning addresses the market issues.
- Take the opportunity to be innovators as opposed to market followers.
- Identify partners to create value to your business.
- Always be customer-led in all of your planning.
- Be prepared to make radical changes for competitive advantage.
- Separate your planning into base business plus a number of development plans.
- Ensure that this document is 'living', ie updated quarterly and rewritten annually.
- Seek out new technologies and apply them.
- Ensure adequate development and training for all senior staff.
- Maintain a focus on purchasing within your business.

BLOCK 4

- The biggest risk in a small business is the risk of doing nothing, because you are only reliant on your base business.
- Right-size your business immediately if you see a reduction in sales, gross margins, cash flow, or fundamental market shifts.
- Plot your monthly sales to understand trends.
- Review your sales processes.
- Look for ineffective management by looking closely at cash flows.
- Examine debtor make-up for poor payers analysis.
- Assess whether suppliers can extend payment terms.
- Measure, review and plan action when such risks are identified.
- Discover the jewels in your business.
- When right-sizing, look at all expenditure, use of IT, process re-engineering and the people in your business.
- During expansion, understand all the funding opportunities and development plans available to you.
- The rapid change management process can help in right-sizing and expansion of your business.

BLOCK 3

- Create a cash-positive environment.
- Control of internal and external costs.
- Presenting the balance sheet.
- Board control.
- Retention of key staff.
- Maintaining supplier relationships.
- Ensure customer focus is key to your business.
- Understand and find your value proposition.
- Ensure your IT is sufficient to compete with your major competitors.
- Control the delivery by 90-day development plans.

building blocks

useful books

Agombar, Fiona (2001) *Endless Energy*, Piatkus Books.

Booher, Dianna (1991) *Executive's Portfolio of Model Speeches*, Prentice Hall.

Drummond, Helga (1991) *Power – creating it and using it*, Kogan Page.

Handy, Charles (1991) *Age of Unreason*, Business Books Ltd.

Handy, Charles (1995) *The Empty Raincoat*, Arrow.

Jeffers, Susan (1997) *Feel the fear and do it anyway*, Rider.

Lintott, David (1990) *Handbook of Company Secretarial Administration*, ICSA.

Roberts, Wess (1993) *Victory Secrets of Attila the Hun*, Bantam Books.

Scrine, A.J. (1990) *Be Your Own Company Secretary*, Kogan Page.

useful addresses and websites

Below is our considered list of contact information.

SMT—Sales and Management Training—
runs a number of specialized courses from the sales beginner to the advanced negotiator. A course for everyone who is serious in business.

SMT
376 Ringwood Road
Poole
Dorset BH12 3LT
Tel: 01202 736747 Mr Joe Windsor

Jay Abraham – American marketing guru par excellence
Courses delivered by audi tape, books and seminars
Nightingale Conent
Long Road
Paignton
Devon TQ4 7BB
Tel: 01803 666100

Institute of Directors – A club for all directors, however small your business. Benchmark, meet, learn or use the HQ building for coffee meetings

IOD
116 Pall Mall
London SW1 5ED
Tel: 020 7839 1233
www.iod.com

BDO Stoy Hayward—National firm of accountants who are genuinely interested in your growing business
Manchester and Liverpool Firm
Cross Street
Manchester M1 5BH
Mr Julien Rye
Tel: 0161 817 3700

Small Business Service – national support for all small businesses in your region.
Tel: 0845 6009006
www.businessadviceonline.org.uk

Business Link
Part of the Small Business Service
www.businesslink.org.uk

British Venture Captai Association
Essex House
12–13 Essex Street
London WC2R 3AA
Tel: 020 7240 3846
www.bca.co.uk

CBI
Centrepoint
103 New Oxford Street
London WC1A 1DU
Tel: 020 7379 7400
www.cbi.org.uk

British Chamber of Commerce
Manning House
22 Carlisle Place
London SW1P 1JA
Tel: 020 7565 2000
www.britishchambers.org.uk

Federation of Small Businesses
2 Catherine Place
Westminster
London SW1E 6HF
Tel: 020 7592 8100
www.fsb.org.uk

Albert Humphrey
Team Action Management
Consultant
1 Randolph Crescent
Little Venice
London W9 1DP

Philip and Sandra Webb
Philip@Webb.co.uk

**Uncontended (Very High Speed)
Dial Up Internet Access To
Subscribe (Free)**
www.webbworlds.co.uk

index